'Letters from the Hills'

The Clodhopper Chronicles

By

Roger Lee Scott

'Letters From the Hills'

ISBN 978-1-4092-8152-8

Foreword

The hills and valleys of middle Tennessee were the geographical playground of my youth. The late 1940's and the decade of the 1950's were my childhood years and they were years of poverty and hardship. The families that were our neighbors were mostly poor and uneducated, and we seemed to be the poorest among the poor. My mother and father were simple sharecroppers, having nothing, materialistically, for most of their lives, and it seemed that the children growing up in our family were destined for the same fate. My older brothers and sisters never made it through elementary school. When I became old enough to enter school, my father began to realize that if I were to have any success in life, I would need an education; therefore, he made sure I went to school.

I had little more than my brothers and sisters, but I persevered with my father's encouragement, that encouragement often coming in a harshest of ways if necessary. Through some miracle, I survived those early years and graduated from high school with honors. I was to go on and finish college, eventually becoming a teacher of high school english.

As a teacher, I would have my students to write stories about characters and instruct them to use various methods to develop the characters. One method was often the use of dialect.

As I read those stories, they brought back memories of the people with whom I had shared my youth. My family and neighbors, the locals in the small towns of middle Tennessee, the people who lived in the remote hills and valleys of my area all became new to me, and I began to see them in a new light. I saw them as an adult from other cultures would see them. Quite often this was in an unflattering way. I'm sure my family and the families around us were much like the characters in this book. They were poor and uneducated for the most part. Their dialect was the dialect of the hills and it often can still be found today in some of the smaller, less affluent communities of rural Appalachia. Though I learned how to speak "proper" English, I love the old hill dialect that I grew up hearing every day of my youth. It is with respect and with a reverence for those times that I have written this book.

None of these characters are real people, but they are based on character types that I knew as a boy and who, later, as an adult, acquired a much greater appreciation of the language and the culture of those rural communities. The stereotypes are there because, though sometimes exaggerated in these chapters, they are a part of our literature and our history. The dialect is written as well as I can remember it, and I apologize if I have erred at times in its usage.

Letter Titles

Dedication

I would like to dedicate this book to my parents and my siblings

Who helped me become who I am and who gave me the means and

support to be successful, to my late wife, Elizabeth,

Who was a daily source of inspiration and encouragement,

And to my dearest of friends, Amelia,

Who helped me to develop the characters in this work

And who served as a guide, advisor, and proofreader.

To all of these who have influenced me so much

And in so many ways,

I thank you.

Recipe for Road Kill

Clem Clodhopper
Rural Route 1
Hogwaller, Arkansaw

Chef Amelia Winslow Blythe
Designin' Wimmen
Trump Tower
New York, New York

Dear Miss Chef Amelia,

My name is Clem Clodhopper, and I lives back in the hills in Hogwaller, Arkansaw. The roads out here ain't nary too good, so's hit's right tiresome to git the mail on sum days. But today I got plumb lucky. I fount this catalog in my mail box which had one of them advertisements. I had Ma to read hit to me, and she said hit had sumpin' to do with Designin' Wimmen. Hit okerred to me that I had knowed some designin' wimmen in my time, so's I thought I would drap a note to you'uns to see if you could holp me with a problem.

Hit's about road kill. Now here in Arkansaw a man likes to shoot his own food. We'uns in the Clodhopper fambly have always been good providers, and my pappy would bust my hide iffen I didn't do the same. But having said that, I ain't no fool nuther, and I jist don't overlook good fortune when hit alights out of the sky. The tother day I fount this possum in the road, and hit was right squishy whar hit had been run over. Now, whens I shoots a squirrel or a ground hog, I can git the bullet out and the meat is still right tasty. Throw hit in a skillet with some lard and cook hit a while and hit's right lairpsome. Ma will fix some cornpone and creases and hit's a meal you can't forgit. But this was a puzzler. I didn't want to jist throw a free meal away, but I was rightly afeered that this ol' possum had been too tenderized fer my tastes. But agin I ain't no waster of vittles, so's I picked hit up right gingerly and dropped hit into a poke and took hit home to Ma.

Now Ma could cook a buzzard and make hit taste like chickin, but this had her puzzled, too. We confabbed a while and reckoned we needed advice on how to cook this thang. We don't own one of them newfangled frigidares, so's I took hit to the sprang and put hit in the water to stay cool until we had heered back from y'all. Of course I left hit in the poke cuz I didn't want hit to spile our dranking water. I'd done all I could so's I tolt Ma to write you and git yore advice. I've heard that you right handy with a skillet, and hit would take Lazarus to raise this thang from the dead and make hit taste right. Jist start me from after hit's skint because I don't have to worry much bout skinning' this thang cuz the skin is pretty much gone. Would hit be better fried or frikasseed? I know a good cook like you would use a lot of lard and mebbe toss in some collard greens. Hits in a lot of pieces so mebbe jist dump hit into a pot and make stew? We'uns is open to all idees you'uns may have. If you would write back soon, we would 'preciate hit so much. Maw and Paw are a little hongry, and I don't like the way they'se lookin' at me.

Wal, I'll back on out of here and wait fer yore answers. Us hill folk ain't big in the way of being beholden to highlanders, but iffen this turns out like I hope, I'll send you a big mess of what we cook up. I know you will like hit. Thanks agin and as my pappy says, "Keep them jacks a'flapping".

Yore friend until the moon shines.

Clem

Amelia's Possum Recipe

January 31, 2002

> Amelia Winslow Blythe
> Designing Women
> Trump Towers
> New York, New York

Clem Clodhopper
Rural Route 1
Hogwallow, Arkansas

Dear Mr. Clodhopper,

Thank you for your inquiry about cooking up a tasty possum. I must say in all my years of culinary school that I have never had such an interesting request which has so challenged my skills and integrity as a chef. However, I think you will find the following recipe most enjoyable and exciting for those with even the most delicate of palates. Recipe is as follows:

1 freshly killed possum...Have your butcher remove the skin and tenderize. (How lucky for you that the tenderizing has already been done for you.)
10 freshly harvested ramps, outside layer removed revealing the best flavor
6 large, good quality beets, trimmed and peeled
½ pound of peas
½ pound of brussel sprouts, outside layers removed and washed thoroughly to remove insects and worms
1 head of celeriac
Dash of Portuguese saffron
Pinch of salt and pepper
36 ounces of fine French wine, preferably a 1969 Nouveau Beaujolais
4 Tbsp of Lungarotti olive oil (first press is best)

In a large, heavy bottomed Dutch oven (I recommend Le Cruset), heat olive oil gently, add ramps, stirring constantly so as not to burn. Place possum tenderloins on top of ramps and sear meat for five minutes on each side releasing the full flavor of the ramps into the meat. Combine remaining ingredients, omitting the Beaujolais. Place in a 400 degree oven for 20 minutes until internal temperature of possum reaches 145 degrees. This will ensure that any unwanted bacteria or parasites will be eliminated. Food safety is very important in this recipe. Remove from oven and let sit for 20 minutes to ensure the meat has time to rest, allowing the meat to remain moist and succulent. Five minutes before serving, add three ounces of the wine to the Dutch oven. This will deglaze the pan and create a most aromatic sauce. Promptly drink the remaining 33 ounces of wine and serve. Bon appetit! Looking forward to further inquiries from a true gourmand.

Sincerely yours,

Chef Amelia Winslow Blythe

Jake's Toe

Clem Clodhopper
Rural Route 1
Hogwaller, Arkansaw

Chef Amelia Winslow Blythe
Designin' Wimmen
Trump Towers
New York, New York

Dear Miss Chef Amelia,

We was shore surprised when we received yore letter. A lot of times folks don't take us serious when we writes to them, but you didn't waste no time a'tall. I knows you has to be right busy inventing all them thangs, so hit pleasured me considerable when you writ back. Afore I gits to the recipe, could you clear my mind on sumthin'? I needs a gadget invented, and I figgered you folks could do hit, being wimmen and all and having a lot of time to set around and thank. Our postman Jake brung the mail today, and he seemed real depressed. His one big toe on his left foot has been hurting him and he can't git no relief. Hit's a hammertoe and hit's got this big old nail that he can't cut with his pocket knife. We'uns have tried larger knifes and soaking hit in water to soften hit and so on, but nuthin ain't working a'tall. We even tried Cuzzin Russell's large hack saw, but hit broke on the first try. We was jist a'wonderin' iffen you had a gadget y'all have invented that would cut that toe nail fer Jake? I wouldn't be too worried but that's the only toe he has on that foot. I don't like to talk about hit much around Jake because he gets all fidgety thanking about his toes, don't you know. You see he lost his toes in a strange way.

Now don't git me wrong. Jake's a good postman, but he does have sum flaws, one of them being he likes a drink now and agin. Wal, one winter two years ago hit got colder than a well digger's bottom hereabouts. Now you know that old saying about rain and snow and

12

dark nights and sich, the mail must go through and so on. Wal, Jake never read that, so sometimes our mail don't go through. Anyways, two winters ago Jake were a'makin' his rounds in the bitter cold, and he set down in our neighbor's barn to rest a tad and have a little nip from the bottle he carries with him. While he were setting there a'drinkin' and a'meditatin', he took off his left shoe to remove a stick that had been worrying him fer some miles on his route. He rubbed his toes a mite to warm them up and took another nip or two. Wal, he jist passed out right thare in the barn. He woke up about three hours later, and his left foot was clean froze. His toon was frostbit so bad that ol' Doc had to remove four of them. The way I sees hit, he should uv jist taken them all and made his foot even because hit's caused him some distress over the years. You see hit's got this one big toe going to the end of the shoe and all this space where them other toes had been. Hit puts a lot of pressure on that one toe which makes hit hurt awful bad. I told him to stuff a sock in it, but for some reason, he took that personal. Anyhow, iffen you could invent something to cut that nail, hit would take some of the pressure off his toe and mebbe we could git our mail more reg'lar.

Wal, I hate wasting yore time talking about Jake and all his trubbles. I'm down to the nub on my pencil, and the lamp is pert near out of oil. Hit's already 7:00 and Ma needs her beauty sleep. Jist betwixt you and me, she can't git that much sleep. Haw, haw, that'll be jist betwixt you and me. Ma and me will try yore suggestions in the recipe you sent me, and I'll git back with you. I can already see a couple of hitches. Hit calls for one head of Celeriac. Now, I thank the Simses across the holler has a boy named Celeriac, but I'm shore he's partial to his head. We don't git along too good with them, but I still would hate to see the boy lose his head. How about throwing in a big ol' hog's head instead, and we could jist invite Celeriac over fer vittles? We tries to git along with our neighbors even though we don't like them. Celeriac's pappy brung me a jug of shine the tother day and had me take a swig. Hit was good enuff, I reckon, but he was mainly trying to show off. He thanks he's got the best shine in the hills, but I knows better and hit jist kills him when folks buys mine instead of his'n. Don't tell ol' J. Edgar that I'm running shine.
Them Fed'ral boys can make hit hard on a feller. I know you won't

tell. Hit's kind of like the code of the hills. You've told us how to cook so now yore part of the fambly and famblies don't tell secrets. Wal, I'll git back on the recipe. But I'm a'goin' to leave Celeriac's head out, iffen you don't keer.

Until the frost bites,

Clem

Crossing Eyes and Dotting T's

February 13, 2002

Dear Miss Chef Amelia,

Hit's Valentine's day tomorry, and I'm shore you has a wing ding of a feast planned, being yore a chef and all. You and yore beau have a good time and don't eat too much chocklit.

Wal, we tried that recipe you sent, but we warn't making any headway a'tall with hit because we didn't have none of them thangs you said to include. Of course, the possum warn't no trubble and the ramps can be got easy enough. God knows Maw loves 'em, bless her soul. Boy, how that woman smells during ramp season! The beets and peas we put into cans during the summer so we has them. The dash of Portuguese saffron was a problem. We had a Portuguese feller dash through these hills once, but I don't know iffen his name were Saffron, and iffen hit had uv been, I don't reckon we could have caught him. He had made the mistake of courting Sue Wilkins who lives in Hootin' Holler, which would have been alright enuff , but her husband warn't too partial to the idee. When he fount out about the affair, he sent that Saffron feller dashing all over these hills with a 12 gauge shotgun as encouragement. And when we got to the French wine, we knew we had problems. French wine would never be fount in the Clodhopper household. Ma's daddy fought in the war alongside the French, and he said he had never seed a more cowardly group of fellers in his life. In one battle the Germans was attacking while a'whoopin' and a'hollerin', and two Frenchies in the trench with him took off like skeered rabbits. Wal, her daddy fit off the Germans pite nite by hisself, and then he run down those Frenchmen and beat them within an inch of their lives. So we ain't real partial to anythang French here. When we goes into town on Satidday night to eat vittles, Maw won't even thank about French fries. That's how hard set she is. So's we jist wound up eating the possum in a stew. Celeriac was glad also. We tolt him about the recipe which called fer his head and he jist laughed. He called us uneddicated is whut he did. Turns out his name ain't Celeriac a'tall, but Cecil. Not only that, but he had gone to college at the local technical school, and he said celeriac was a type of celery. Now, I know I ain't smart but I don't thank a boy should be uppity around his betters. I'm almost sorry we didn't use his head since it don't seem to be a'doing him no good a'tall.

Miss Amelia you are a Godsend. I want to thank you fer sending the gadget fer Jake's toe nail. Hit kinda looked like Maw's pruning shears, but hit was the sharpest doohickey we had ever saw. Jake applied hit to the toe nail and that thang popped off like a ripe melon from the vine. So's he's a'moving a little better now, and we should be gitting our mail on a more reg'lar basis. You know how postmen love to talk. Wal, Jake was telling us about a boy on his route who had sum problems with his eyes. This is the Ledbetter boy who lives down from the Simses who have the boy who we thought was Celeriac, but was actually Cecil. Anyhow, the Ledbetter boy had crost his eyes too much when he was little, and they had come to be stuck thataway. The boy can't see a thang in front of him, but he has the vision of a hawk to the sides. Now, this wouldn't be a bad thang, but he keeps a'runnin' into thangs in front of him, and his head is a mess of bumps and bruises, don't you know. His maw is real upset about the sitiation and don't know whut to do. She's afraid the boy is going to fall offen a cliff and kill hisself. I allowed how she might put a patch over one eye and that could make the tother straighten out. She tried it right enuff, but the poor boy started walking in circles until he became so dizzy that he actual did tumble off a cliff. Miss Ledbetter ain't speaking to me right now, and I thought you might be able to help. I know I'se asking a lot from you and yore designin' wimmen, but you gals seem to know everythang. If there's a solution that's gadgetical, please let us know.I know yore time costs money and we kin pay. We ain't freeloaders after all. The Clodhoppers are a pridesome group, and we pay our own way. If hit's going to cost a couple of dollars to straighten out the Ledbetter boy, we kin afford hit. In the meantime the Ledbetter boy is crossing his eyes and dotting his t's. Haw, haw. Sometimes I amuse myself.

Yores til the jar flies.

Clem

Amelia's Solution to Crossed Eyes

February 23, 2002

Chef Amelia Winslow Blythe
Designing Women
Trump Towers
New York, New York

Mr. Clem Clodhopper
Rural Route 1
Hogwallow, Arkansas

Dear Mr. Clodhopper,

What a dilemma for young Master Ledbetter! We at Designing Women do not profess to be skilled in ocular technology, and what we advocate might go against all professional ethics in that medical field. But since you lack access to trained ophthalmologists or institutions there in your area that could help you, I will just rely on common sense measures and put this into terms that you and your family will understand. It is drastic and I hate to think of that small boy being teased more than he already is, but here is one solution. Take several good strong rubber bands and pull his hair as tightly as you can to the sides. He might look like a small girl in pigtails, but I can assure you that if they are tight enough, his eyes will return to normal. As an added measure, each day have the lad to focus on an object in front of him, gradually trying to bring each eye into play on the object. Each time he does this, make the focus session a little longer until the eye muscles are trained to pull the eyes forward. Your idea of the patch over one eye will work also. Just don't let him walk around while he is wearing it. We don't want any more harm to come to him. I hope this will help you to patch (pardon the pun) things up with Mrs. Ledbetter. While he is concentrating on this rehabilitation, let him listen to rap music. That should speed up the process substantially. Just a bit of humor.

Thank you Mr. Clodhopper for your confidence in our organization. If we can be of further help, let us know.

Chef Amelia Winslow Blythe

Uncle Henry and the Pill

March 4, 2002

Dear Miss Chef Amelia,

   You gals are a fount of knowledge. Us Clodhoppers is so glad we fount yore ad in the catalogue. Youn'ses at Designin' Wimmen have been awfully nice to a fambly of jist plain hill folk that y'all never met. The Ledbetter chile will benefit from all this wisdom I am shore. We was uncertain on sum of the words you used, like opthamolojist and sich, and I'm not shore I want to send the boy to no institution. Uncle Henry was in one of them places once, and he jist never recovered. Uncle Henry liked to hang around down in the flatlands alot and carouse or jist loafer. Now I ain't saying he's a good fer nothing, but work and Uncle Henry are words you don't see together reg'lar. Wal, Uncle Henry one day was a'drinkin' outside the town drug store. They has some nice benches out there on the porch, and Uncle Henry was partaking of the comfort of one of them there benches. He'd take a sip now and agin and jist pass the time of day with any pretty gal that sashayed by. Wal, a lady came out of the drug store with a package. She was a'fumblin' with some item and hit came open, and a large tablet fell on the porch unbeknownst to her. She jist walked on and Uncle Henry picked hit up. He thought hit was peppermint candy, and he wondered how that might give the whiskey a little more nip. He stuck that thang on his tongue and took a big swig of that elixir, and whut happened next is still talked about around here in Hogwaller. Suddenly, all manner of foam jist started spilling out of his mouth. He was a'coughin' and a'spittin' and the foam was jist a'rollin'.
   Wal, everyone came a'runnin'. A couple of Hootin'Holler boys grabbed Uncle Henry and held him down. Eveybody thought he was having one of them seezures and somebody said to grab his tongue so's he wouldn't bite hit off, but nobody wanted to stick their hand in

Uncle Henry's mouth. So he jist kept on a'foamin' and a'strugglin' with the Hootin' Holler boys until he jist plumb wore hisself out. Betwixt the alcohol and the excitement, he jist passed out. Now, nobody knew whut to do. Ol' Doc Whittaker said to send him to the institution in Little Rock to have his head examined. He thought sure Uncle Henry was out of his gourd.

The upshot is that they examined Uncle Henry's head and fount nothing, but the stay there had upset him so much that he was never the same. So now you can see why we'uns don't cotton to institutions. But gitting back to the Ledbetter boy, we tried the rubber bands on the head, but the boy looked so awful that we feared he would be scarred fer life, and we figgered being crossed eyed would be a heap better than having the boy thank he was a gal. So's we gave up on that idee. We didn't know about the rap music cause nobody was sure whut hit was. Pa suggested rapping on the wall and playing the banjo whilst the boy was sleeping, but the poor chile never got no rest, and this jist seemed to make the eyes worser. So's we jist decided to let nature take hit's course. With his luck, maybe some horse will kick him in the head or he'll take another tumble when he has one of them dizzy spells and hit'll jar his eyeballs back into place. We can only hope.

Ma has a woman problem she wants to ask you about, but I told her to wait a mite. We'uns have imposed on you'uns too much already. I'll let you rest yore brains and write agin later. Until then remember what my pappy always says, "You can lead a horse to water but a crosseyed chile often goes astray". Pappy is known around these parts as quite a philosopher. Wal, hit's time to go slop the hawgs. And after I git through feeding the fambly, I guess I'll feed the pigs. Haw, haw.

Yores till the eye bawls,

Clem

Amelia's Woodpecker Dilemma

March 15, 2002

Dear Mr. Clodhopper,

I was most pleased to get your missive from the great state of Arkansas. I hope everything is fine in my cousin's state. My cousin just happens to be former President Bill Clinton. Yes, I know his reputation was besmirched just a little by that Monica person but we should not be judgmental. I can assure you that if any of your family need any help, he's only a phone call away.

Now, I would like you to know that, like yourself, I was not born with a silver spoon in my mouth. I am a pioneer woman who can fend for herself. However, I have a dilemma. Since I am dispensing my expertise in your direction, perhaps you can return the favor on your end. I have five woodpeckers destroying my house. I do not know what to do and I have tried everything. I even purchased a Wal-Mart special air rifle to try and get rid of them. Although I have shot weapons before and I have considerable skill with them, unfortunately, the laws in our state prevent me from performing mayhem on these creatures. Do you have any suggestions on how to get rid of them? I await your correspondence.

Chef Amelia Winslow Blythe

Ma Clodhopper's Letter

March 25, 2002

Dear Miss Chef Amelia,

My name is Clara May Clodhopper, and I am Clem's ma which you have been receiving mail from of late. Clem is a good boy with a square head on his shoulders. He likes gadgetical thangs and has been mighty impressed with the advice you have been a'givin' him. I tolt him I had a problem that you folks at Designin' Wimmen might holp me with, but he said I shouldn't be worrying you with my trubbles. I reckon his'n are more important than mine. He said fer me to try Dear Abby, but I don't reckon I'll ask her. Effie Sue Mayberry down in Hootin' Holler writ to her once fer some advice, and hit didn't turn out no good a'tall.

It seems that Effie Sue's husband Harley had been a'runnin' around on her with a couple of wimmen from Possum Crick, and Effie Sue fount out about hit. To beat hit all, the wimmen he was a'seein' were sisters and didn't seem to mind that each of them was chewing on the same chicken laig. Wal, don't you know Dear Abby said fer Effie Sue to plop down one of them ultimaters and brang the thang to a head. So's Effie Sue one night when they was a'sittin' down to supper told Harley she knowed whut he was a'doin', and hit was either her or the sisters. If he liked sev'ral wimmen at one time, mebbe he ort to join one of them communes in Californee. Wal, to beat hit all, the next morning Harley was gone. He had packed his clothes during the night and taken off to Californee. He hadn't knowed about them communes, and he thought he'd like to give them a try. He didn't even bother to take the sisters. So now Effie Sue and the sisters have become good friends and are jist waiting fer the day Harley comes back home with his tail betwixt his legs. They've got a real homecomin' waiting fer him. Anyways, you see why Dear Abby might not be the answer to my problem.

Afore I git to the problem that I want to chew on, I need to git to yore letter you sent to us. You asked Clem fer some learning on how to get shed of a woodpecker that was a' tearin' up yore house. Now, you have been awfully good to give advice, so I will try to return the favor.

We'uns here at the Clodhopper household don't shoot anythang we can't eat. Ma Nature is kind to us and we want to return the favor. Most critters is jist trying to survive. You didn't say whut yore house is made of, but iffen hit's wood, a woodpecker is jist natural drawn to hit. That's how hit got hit's name, Hit's jist pecking for insects. Do you think you got insects in yore house? Paw will go out and shoo them peckers away ever now and then, but they jist come back. We figger with all the holes already in the house, a few more here and there ain't gonna matter. We jist git more fresh air thataway. Some folks here in these parts considers woodpeckers to be good luck, and I like that idee cuz since them knotheads have been around, all kinds of nice thangs have happened to us, including gitting to know a nice highlander like yoreself. I would figger out whut woodpeckers are afeered of and hang one or two of them around. Mebbe an owl or hawk. Or mebbe you could spray some kind of bad smelling mixings in the areas where they are a'peckin'. Paw uses skunk oil but you might be more partial to some smelly stuff you can git at yore local mercantile. Anyways, good luck.

Miss Chef Amelia, I'm a straightforward woman. When a chikin' neck needs wranging, I'm the woman who can do hit. When thar's a problem, I face it and chew fat or die. So here goes. I'm pite nigh fifty-two years old, and my husband Clayton ain't paid me one of them conjugal visits in quite a while. Now a woman at fifty-two ain't dead by a long shot. I'm jist now beginning to feel my oats. The children are gone 'cepting for Clem who keeps drapping by to git me to help him write letters. The house is empty and there is plenty of chances for some activity under the sheets, if you know whut I mean. I bought this sexy negligee the last time I was in Smith's Mercantile, and a few nights ago I tried hit on. I thought I looked right fetching. Wal, that night I fixed Clayton a wing ding of a supper and set it on the table. I turnt the lights down low and put Roy Acuff on the crank Victrola. The trap was set, and I was feeling purty good about my prospects. When Clayton set down to vittles, I turned on the Victrola and Roy was sanging "The Great Speckled Bird," which is only one of

23

Clayton's favorites of all time. I sashayed into the room in that negligee and set down in my cheer across the table. Wal, Clayton never looked up. He was a'wolfing down them vittles and never paid me no mind a'tall. So's I harrumphed real loud to git his attention, but he jist kept right on eating. I could have gotten more attention if I had uv been a big old lump of bacon in the other cheer. I harrumphed agin, and he looked up and asked me to pass him sum collard greens.

Wal, that was hit. I jumped up and said, "Clayton, you git into that bedroom. We'uns is going to know each other in a Biblical way." Clayton ain't much on the Bible, but he could see chapter and verse on my face, so he scurried into the bedroom. I thought that everythang was a'rollin' right along, but somethang warn't quite right. Clayton's magic wand warn't producing no magic, if you gits my drift. I asked him whut was a'matter, but he was too ashamed to tell me. I had read somethang about this very thang in the *Farmer's Almanac*. Hit's call impotency. Now, I've heered that thar are thangs that a man can take fer this. We don't git much information here in the hills on this kind of problem, so's I'm askin' you to send me whut pamplets you have on the subject and maybe some advice iffen you know wimmen who've had the same trubbles. I know this may not be in yore line of work, but yore still wimmen, and us wimmen need to stick together. Thank you for yore time and good luck with yore woodpecker.

Hoping for a wood pecker,

Clara May Clodhopper

Amelia's Advice to Ma Clodhopper

April 6, 2002

Dear Mrs. Clodhopper,

I have to admit when I first read your recent letter, I was very nonplussed about how to respond. Let me say that the problem you described concerning your husband is not unusual. When a man reaches a certain age, he does not produce as much testosterone, and other factors, such as diet and exercise and even certain diseases, can dampen his ardor in the boudoir. I am not a married woman, but I do have some expertise in this area, having read many articles and journals on the subject. Having friends who like to talk about their sexual exploits doesn't hurt either. Let me say that you are on the right track. The way to a man's heart is through his stomach. Cooking one of his favorite meals, wearing sexy clothing, lighting candles, and playing mood music are all vital to setting the atmosphere for romance. Though I personally do not like Roy Acuff, if that is what he likes to hear, by all means play his music. Have you ever tried Brahms or Tchaikovsky or any of the other great classical composers? Perhaps Frank Sinatra or Harry Belafonte would stir his passion.

Do you take time during the day to talk to each other? Hold hands? Ask him about his day? All these things will tend to bring you closer as a couple and eventually lead to your ultimate goal, which is to get him into the bedroom. However, if there really is a physical problem involved, which prevents his "magic wand", as you say, from performing, perhaps a visit to your local physician is in order. He may be embarrassed to admit his problem, but it is in your best interest to get him help by any means. Your marital harmony is at stake. There are drugs such as Viagra that will help, but they need to be prescribed by a doctor. Counseling is often effective. It will be difficult on your part to get him to submit to the idea of a third party being involved in the problem, but it has proven to be effective. Again, let me emphasize that I am not an expert in this field though I do pride myself on my knowledge in this area. I will be interested to hear what you decide to do.

In regard to the woodpecker that is destroying my house, I do appreciate so much your advice. I do not want to kill the creature. The house is not wood, as you assumed, but stucco. I do not know why any self-respecting bird would want to peck a hole in stucco. Perhaps the repellant you suggested will work. I will give it a try.

Sincerely yours,

Chef Amelia Winslow Blythe

Clem's Educational Woes

April 10, 2002

Dear Miss Chef Amelia,

I learned that my maw writ you a letter. I hope she didn't waste yore time with a bunch of rambling. She can be right tiresome when she gits on one of her touchy subjects. One of them subjects is Paw. They don't seem to be hitting it off too good right now. With all us children gone, they don't have nobody to fuss on but theirselves. With us around, we was always gitting the bumps and bruises and Paw kinda laid low, but now that we's gone, he's taking a tongue lashing about ever day. Paw says he jist wishes Maw would throw a skillet or a hammer at him. It wouldn't hurt near as much. If she's asking for advice, and you got time, holp her out. I know Paw would 'preciate hit.

Miss Chef Amelia, I knows that I are a'loading up yore plate with a lot of my problems, but they jist seem to appear like flies and are a whole lot more worrisome. I knows I'm not an eddicated man, and hit bothers me that I may never make nothing of myself. You gals at Designin' Wimmen are smart folks, and I git a bit flustered when I starts to write and can't put all the words in order. I got them in my head like I want them, but when I goes to write them down, they don't come out the way I am a'thanking. Oh, I had a pretty fair eddication. I done went through third grade so I can cipher and spell and do sums a little, but while that's good for hereabouts, it ain't gonna git me a good job in yore world. I'm nigh on to thirty now and thangs ain't a'getting no better in prospects fer me. Birdie Jones down the holler is about my age, and he went to a technical school all the way over in Asheville, North Carolina. Now he has a good job in a factory in Raleigh putting motors together for GM. He's a'makin' money hand over fist and he's talked about round here as a big success story. He got out of the hills and is doing good. He's even sending money back to his ma and pa, and they've bought a big satellite dish and one of them television sets. Me and Pa went over to watch hit the tother night, and hit were a sight.

We seen something called RAW. It was a rasslin' match and, boy howdy, they was a'throwin' each other all over the place. Chairs was a'flyin', bodies was a'crashin', and they was a'pointin' and a'gesturin'. But to beat hit all, a woman came into the rang and whopped a man over the head with a cheer. She had pert nigh nothing on and was mussled up like Mattie Rawlings who lives up the hill a ways. Mattie ordered from a catalogue one of them machines whut builds up yore mussles. We never knew whut she wanted to do that fer, but she was shore a success. We fount out later that she had joined a circus and performed feets of strength in front of large crowds. Anyhow, this woman on television was jist whaling away with this cheer, and anuther woman jumps in the rang and starts whaling away on her. Now you got men and women jist whomping on each other and even the crowd gits into the act with a bunch of people trying to git in the rang and take part. Birdie's paw was jist gitting so excited watching all this that he was a'jumpin' up and down and a'givin' them all whut fer in a language that Maw won't let me repeat. Anyhow, I thank I'll go back over next Sattiday night. I want to see a little more of them wimmen fighting each other. Some mention was made of wimmen on an upcoming show doing some mud rasslin'. Do you know whut that is? I may want to watch hit.

Now I done gone and lost my train of thought. Wimmen do that to me. Oh, yeah, I was reckoning my eddication was lacking a bit and a'wonderin' if you have any suggestions. Here in the hills I don't have much of a way to make money. I needs a job to make money to git an eddication, but I have to have an eddication to git a job and hit takes money to git the eddication. Hit's one of them varicose circles that I've heered about. I admire yore upbranging and eddicated ways. I strongly reckon my brain would be better iffen I had the learning you do. I know Maw has asked you fer some advice on somethang or tother, so my trubbles can wait awhile. My brain ain't going nowhere. Whutever you can come up with I'm a'willing to listen to. I would hate to leave Hogwaller cuz I thank Maw and Paw need me right now, but I have my own life to git on with. Thank you for yore time. Yores till the book worms. Haw, haw. With my sense of humor, there's gots to be a school willing to take me on.

Yore devoted servant.

Clem

Great Literary Works vs. "Rasslin'"

April 21, 2002

Dear Clem,

I hope you don't mind if I call you Clem. We have corresponded enough that I feel we are friends. Yes, I have discussed some items with your mother. I don't know that anything will be resolved soon, but hopefully she has a basis for a start in the right direction. I found it very interesting that you want to further your education. That shows a lot of initiative and foresight on your part. One needs to take stock of his situation and weigh the pros and cons concerning where his life is at present and if that is where he wants to be. You mentioned, I believe, that you are around thirty years of age? If that is true, then you are getting a late start on a career. Personally, my career is well established and I am no older than you are. My prospects for advancement are very good, if I do say so myself. But let us talk about your education which was the crux of your letter.

First of all, get away from the television and your "rassling" programs. They will rot your mind. You must begin reading. I believe you told me you went through the third grade. Books like **Moby Dick, Gone with the Wind,** and **War and Peace** might interest you. They are classic books and on a level you can read. Instead of concentrating on "wimmen", focus your attention on great works. Go to art museums. Do you have any great concert auditoriums there in Hogwallow? Next, you must get a job to fund your education. Work part time while you take courses in your area of choice. There are hardship loans available to underprivileged students. You may have to get a GED in order to get into an institution of higher learning. Do you know what your IQ is? Perhaps you are intelligent enough to be promoted several grades in school. Counselors in your local high school in Hogwallow can help you.

Lastly, get out of Hogwallow! The first step in any type of higher education is to get away from home and the bad influences there. You will be on your own, making your own decisions, and charting your own course to success. You can never be successful as long as you stay tied to one spot, especially if that spot holds no prospects for you.

I hope I have been of some help. Let me know of any decisions that you might make in the near future. I feel like you are a part of my extended family and I am interested in your decisions.

With warm regards,

Chef Amelia Winslow Blythe

Clem and *Moby Dick*

April 30, 2002

Miss Chef Amelia,

Wal, I have never been so excited! I feel like I've eat two moon pies and drunk three red drinks all at one time. Hit's pert nigh like one of them pep rallies at school afore a ball game. I remember gitting so excited when them little cheerleaders from Hogwaller Grammar School would come out with them pom poms and stir everybody up. They'd jiggle around and the crowd would yell and ever time a hoop was scored, they would jist go into a frenzy. I didn't play in grade school because of my asthma. I couldn't have played anyways because I was only in the third grade and you had to be in the fifth grade to play. My eddication was nipped afore I got that fur along. But I remember the excitement, and that's the way I feel after reading yore letter agreeing with me whut with me wanting to git more learning.

I will need some clearing up on a few of yore directions. I ain't so good at reading or writing as you can tell from my letters. Our liberry in Hogwaller is awfully pore in books. Thay's about fifteen books in the whole liberry, but I heered that Mrs. Watson in Hootin' Holler passed away and left five goodun's in honor of her passing. Now I don't know whut they are, but iffen any of them are the books you talked about, I will give them a look see. I heered that **Moby Dick** was about a fish and I do like to fish, so I may give that'un a try. My good buddy Skeeter Thompson and me went fishing a short time ago and hit was an adventure. Now I ain't much of a dranking man, but Skeeter likes to tipple now and agin. He brung some strong elixir with him on this trip and stayed close to that bottle purty much all day. We had jist pushed our boat out into the water and was gitting ready to drown a worm when Skeeter stood up to take off his coat. Wal, he waren't all that stiddy on his feet and he started a'rockin' back and forth. Before I could do anythang about hit, he fell head over heels into the water. He came up a'sputterin' and a'coughin'. We struggled fer a spell, but we finally got him back into the boat. He had lost his bottle and the cold water seemed to sober him a mite, so we jist continued to fish. Fishing is a quiet sport, and Skeeter had purty much skeered all the fish in the lake away, so I got into a talking way and tolt him about me wanting to git an eddication. He jist kinda smile and said he was happy jist the way he is. Some folks are thataway. Skeeter didn't go looking for work, and work never fount him. He was content in his own way jist to sit on a bank and fish and smoke a pipe or sit on his front porch and whittle. He said that's what guv'ment checks are fer, so's a man could enjoy life without working. But somehow, Miss Chef Amelia, I think thar's got to be more. Yore letter has me lathered up like an overworked plow mule.

Gitting a job in Hogwaller won't be easy. What with the economy the way hit is, jobs are scarcer than hen's teeth. The only skill I have hain't called fer much. I can play guitar and a juice harp like you won't believe. At all the dances, I'm called upon to play. Paw plays the jug, I play the juice harp, and Joe Conley plays a mean fiddle. Is there any call for guitar or juice harp playing where you are? Leaving Hogwaller ain't something I figgered on doing fer a while, but you say I need to, and I guess yore right. All the fellers who've left here have done much better than I has. Hit's hard leaving family when they needs you. Hit's somethang I'll have to thank on a spell. Ma ain't gonna like hit one bit. Whut did yore ma say when you left fer the city? Yep, I'll have to chew on this a spell and figger out how to tell Ma whut I'm a'thinkin' about doing. Paw always says, "Figgering ain't hard as long as I got all my fingers and toes." Wal, I could wind up like Jake, our postman who lost his toes, and have nothing to count on.

Mulling hit over,

Clem

A Shotgun Wedding

May 7, 2002

Dear Miss Chef Amelia,

I am so glad that you consider me yore friend. I ain't never had no close woman friend afore. It's jist fine filen you call me Clem, but I have to call you Miss Chef Amelia since you are my better, being college eddicated and all. Maybe when my brain catches up to yorn, I can call you by yore first name. I hain't got no problems to discuss this time, so's you can rest yore brain on that account. I thought I would jist tell you some thangs that are a'goin' on in the hills.

Hit's gitting close to sprang here, and there's a lot of going's on going on. Jist this past week we had a doozie of a ruckus in the Tucker household. Hit seems that Annabelle Tucker has been seeing the Sims boy. You know the one whut we thought was called Celeriac back when you was a'tellin' me how to cook the possum and whut actually is Cecil and not Celeriac a'tall. Wal, Cecil and his higher eddication has got into a world of trubble, and I don't reckon his books can git him out of hit nuther. He has been squiring Annabelle on the sly unbeknownst to her paw. Now old man Tucker is no one to be trifled with, and he fount out that Cecil and Annabelle had been sneaking out at night and sparking down by the crick. Here in the hills, hit's tradition fer a boy to come calling and talk to the paw when he wants to squire a gal around. Now Cecil thought that since he is older than Annabelle that mebbe the old man wouldn't let his little girl go sparking with him. Annabelle is only sixteen, don't you know, and new to the ways of the world. Cecil, on the tother hand, has seed the elephant, being right hansome and well eddicated, so's they reckoned hit would be good to keep it on the sly whut with her paw being overly pertective. Ole man Tucker got wind of whut was goin' on and laid in wait fer Cecil to show up one night. When Cecil crept out of the bushes and did his bird call to signal Annabelle, hit was old man Tucker who answered the call. Hit wasn't with a kiss nuther. He pointed a 12 guage shotgun filled with double ought shot at the boy, and ole Cecil nearly keeled over with fright. Ole man Tucker told Cecil in no uncertain words that he was a'goin' to have to marry his daughter. He said everyone in the hills knowed whut was a'goin' on and his fambly reputation was at stake. The only honorable way to git out of hit was to git hitched, and he was a'gonna see that it was done or there would be one less Sims in the holler. The next day the bans were printed, and they's to be married next week.

Now all that is well and good, but thar's a problem in that regard. The preacher will be Reverend Billings, the preacher down in Hootin' Holler. Reverend Johnson, who was a'goin' to do the honors, got ill sudden like. Hogwallow is still a'talking about hit. We was at Sunday meeting this past Sunday and everythang was a'going as usual. Reverend Johnson was warming to his sermon whut was about puttin' a little more in the collection plate each Lord's day. Hit seems that hit was becoming a habit for some members to go out on Sattiday night and blow all their money on whiskey and cards and then come in on Sunday morning and leave a IOU in the collection plate. So's Brother Johnson was saying as to about how the Lord don't take no IOU's in heaven. The Lord's cut comes first and He expects a tenth of that welfare check ever month. Wal, you could see some ole boys squirming in their pews as the sermon got hotter and hotter. Brother Johnson was a'stomping, and a'yelling, and preaching fire and damnation to raise the rafters. He had jist begin a series of tuh-huttins when suddenly his face turnt bright red and he jist keeled over right there in the pulpit. Well, all was quiet fer a second whilst everyone was digesting whut had happened, and then there was a great stirring as people rushed up to the pulpit. Hit seems that Reverend Johnson had worked up one of them coronas, and he had to be taken to Little Rock. He's all right. He's gonna need some bed rest for a long time. I don't reckon he will collect on them IOU's. Anyhow, Reverend Billings will do the Cecil and Annabelle wedding. I hope he keeps hit low key. We can't afford to lose another preacher anytime soon.

Wal, that's all I got to report. Hit's kind of like one of them soap oprys around here every oncet a while. Write back whens you git's the time. Until then. I remain yore servant.

Yores til the wedding bells,

Clem

Amelia and Questions on Life

May 17, 2002

Dear Clem,

Your stories are delightful. Our worlds are very different; yet there seem to be so many common threads that lead me to believe people are pretty much the same the world over. We all survive in spite of the hardships thrown at us. We all want to be successful, regardless of what our walk of life is. We all want to be loved and to be respected for who we are, and, based on your stories, weird things can happen to all of us at any time. Life doesn't hold any guarantees. We have the present only. We can plan and hope and prepare as best we can for the future, but we don't know what that future will hold regardless of how well prepared we are. We are all pawns to fate. Who knew Brother Johnson would have a coronary? He hadn't planned for that. Who knew that Cecil would get married whether he wanted to or not. Sometimes, things are planned for us by fate or just by other people. I'm almost thirty and I have a good career plan which is progressing nicely, but something seems to be missing. Most of my friends are married and have families already. It's difficult to balance a career with a marriage and family. It's something I think about more and more often as I see thirty approaching.

What are your plans for a family? Have you thought about it like I have? Obviously, you're concerned about your education and advancing yourself in a career. I'm sure that are many pretty girls there in Hogwallow or in Hootin' Holler that are looking for a thoughtful man who is a good provider. But perhaps that is too personal and something you don't want to talk about. I'll not ask any more questions, but I do like receiving your letters. They give me a perspective on a type of life that I had not known existed. I guess I've been too sheltered up to this point. Keep me attuned to how your job hunt and your educational pursuits are progressing.

Your friend,

Chef Amelia

Clem at McDonald's

May 30, 2002

Dear Miss Chef Amelia,

I was right pleased to git yore letter the tother day. I'm jist now replying cause I have to wait and git Maw to help me read hit. Betwixt the two of us, we wade through hit and figure out whut yore saying. Boy howdy, you know some big words. I'se started on one of the books you tolt me I might like. Hit's called *Moby Dick*. That is shore some big book. I bet the whale ain't much bigger. Iffen I can git through hit a'tall, hit'll be next winter afore I will know if ole Ahab caught that big ol' fish. Are you shore I can read this thang? You have a mite more belief in whut I can do than most people.

I'm glad yore career is doing so good. As soon as I got yore first letter, I knowed you was a high-toned woman. You'uns at Designin' Wimmen do a lot fer folks. I reckon you treat all folks alike cause I ain't never had nobody to be so nice to me. I bet the men thar air jist waiting in line. I hope you find someone good natured to spend yore time with. The troubles I have had with the female sex in Hogwaller has soured me a tad, but I hain't got time to git into that now. Mebbe later when yore tender ears can take hit. I went down into the flatlands yestiddy, and I started looking fer a job like you said fer me to do. What with the economy being bad, there hain't much out there. I finally stopped in a place called McDonald's and asked them iffen they needed any holp. I'm not shore whut they do, but they's got the biggest yaller sign you've ever seed. I figgered they had to be mighty important to have a sign like hit. So's I went in and talked to a man they called the manager. He listened to me whilst I explained why I needed a job, and he jist nodded his haid whilst I was a'talkin'. They is a happy bunch in that place. All the time that manager was asking his questions, they was a laughing to beat the band. Since I have a good sense of humor, I could see myself a'workin' thar. Wal, the manager took me to a table and we set down, and he started asking a lot of personal questions like whut grade did I go to in school, whut are sum

36

of my hobbies, who's the President of the United States, is my maw and paw kin to each other, and on and on.

My head begin to hurt after a while, and he give me a sandwich and one of them fountain drinks, and I soon started to feel better. They give me something called a Big Mac, but hit warn't any bigger than Bubba Hopkins' burgers. Bubba will kill a big ol' deer now and agin and grind some of hit up to make into patties. He'll slap them thangs down into a big pit and let them cook a while and put them betwixt some of his maw's cathead biscuits and, lawdy, they's good. But the manager said that Big Mac was one of his best sellers, so's I guess he knows whut he's a'doin'.

The manager said he was a little concerned about my verbal skills. I warn't sure what he meant, and he tolt me hit was the way I talked. I didn't thank hit was all that differnt. All the folks up in Hogwaller understands me jist fine. I tolt him that I was a'goin' to improve myself by going back to school, so's he didn't have to worry none about my talking skills. He said that he didn't want folks who work thar to draw attention to theirselves, so's he reckoned that he couldn't hire me. The young man who give me my food said he was awful sorry I didn't git the job, but I really had a hard time making out whut he was a'sayin' with that big silver ball he had stuck into his tongue. He talked a lot to his friend who seemed to have trubble making out what he was a'sayin' jist like me. I guess he had ear trubble. He had a big ole round ring of some sort in the lobes of his ears. They had pretty nigh stretched the lobes down to his jaw. They probably warn't distractions, but I had a hard time not looking at them thangs. Pappy's ole snout rings that he uses on his hawgs warn't that big.

Wal, I guess hit's best I didn't git hired. I don't thank I could work fer a bunch of folks whut lies. They's a sign outside that says one billion served. I don't know much about numbers, but that would have to have four or five zeros on the end of hit. They's not that many people in Hogwaller and Hootin' Holler toted up. I heered that there is a job at Sam Perkin's lumber mill, so's I'm a'headin' over that way to try and get hit. Wish me luck and I look toward hearing back from you.

Yore job hunting pal,

Clem

People in High Places

June 10, 2002

Dear Clem,

I was so angry after I read your letter about the disastrous experience at McDonald's. Your spirit must be shattered after such an inauspicious start to finding a job. Those cretins should not be allowed to run a pig pen, and most certainly not a McDonald's restaurant. You poor man! I will personally write to the McDonald's corporate office and demand that they look into the incident immediately. Mr. Bill Clinton, the former President of the United States, is my cousin. I will call him about McDonald's terrible hiring practices.

Even after such a start, you still persevere. Yes, I think working at a saw mill might be good for a short time. I imagine the men who work at lumber mills are quite strong. I can see you swinging an axe, getting into a rhythmic motion. Your muscles rippling beneath the torn and sweaty shirt you are wearing. The perspiration on your body glistening in the sun as it runs down your chest and stomach into…Oh, my goodness! I seem to have lost track of the point I was making. What I meant to say is that while manual labor will not improve your mind, it will be a temporary reprieve from the doldrums of inactivity. The ladies will find you to be much more of a catch if you have a steady job. Even though you seem reluctant to talk of your past romances, you must tell me about some of those experiences that have soured you on the feminine sex…uh, I mean feminine gender. My! My! I do not know what is wrong with me. I must be coming down with the flu. I suddenly feel that I need a cool drink of water. I will have the staff nurse to check my temperature. I'm sure it's only temporary.

I will close now and I hope your job hunt is a success.

Your friend,

Chef Amelia.

Clem and the Waffle House Incident

June 18, 2002

Dear Chef Amelia,

I hope yore feeling better. Yore last letter was kind of worrisome. City wimmen seem to be upset by katch colds and thangs more oftener than mountain wimmen. I know yore a delicate thang so don't let some bug git into yore system. Wal, you asked me about my romantical doings and I spect I have to oblige since we are friends. I ain't had much luck with the wimmen folk in this area. I expect I am one of them people who is hard to please. I ain't askin' much. She needs to be as smart as me in book larning and have most of her teeth. I don't want no snuff dipper ner drinker ner smoker. Them's vices I jist can't tolerate in a woman which throws out pert near all the wimmen in Hogwaller.

The first date I had with a woman come about when my buddy Claypool Pennywell and me went to Little Rock last summer to the annual cow and hog show. We stayed in one of them swanky Motel 6's whut had running water and indoor toilets and even one of them television sets. We had jist settled in when Claypool got the call of nature, and he went into the bathroom to answer hit. He came out all concerned because the water was dripping awful bad in the sink, and he was afeered he would be blamed. He called down to the desk clerk. "I gotta leak in the sink," he says to the clerk. The clerk didn't seemed concerned and he jist says, "Well, go ahead." Wal, Claypool felt he had done his duty and went about his bissness.

That night we went to a place called the Waffle House for vittles. Hit was right acrost from the Motel 6. Claypool and me didn't have no car, having rid on one of them Greyhound buses the 100 miles to Little Rock. So's we jist walked over to the Waffle House and set down. Wal, it was busier than a cat's tail in a room full of rocking cheers. Them waitresses was calling out orders and them cooks was slanging sausages and bacon and eggs to beat the band. Now, Claypool is pretty well off money wise. His paw left him the fambly bissness in

Hogwaller which is the local feed and grain store. So's he says to git anythang on the menu. Hit's on him. I see's a pitcher of jist whut I want. Hit's three aigs, with sausage and bacon, home fries, grits, biskits, gravy, and I throwed in some waffles fer good measure. I didn't hanker to eat too much and feel all bloated later. The waitress brung us some coffee and struck up a palaver with Claypool, but I could tell she was a'sizing me up with her eyes.

"You boys new in town?" She asks all polite like.

"We's here for the cow and hog show," says Claypool, as smooth as you please.

She puts her hand on her hip and smiles real big and says, "Wal, I could tell you were some high rollers."

Now, I ain't sure whut she meant by that, but ol' Claypool jist chuckled and said, "We hain't got nuthin' to do tonite iffen yore not busy after work. Whut's yore name?"

Wal, to make a long story tolerable, she says her name is Ida Sue Maxwell and she had a friend that Claypool might like to meet.

"Yore friend don't talk much," she says and looks at me like I was the last pork chop at a pig roast. "How would you like to see me after work?"

I gulps real big and spills about half the coffee on my lap, but Claypool sets the meeting up and we gits our meal and eats hit.

We meets them gals after they git off from work, and Claypool and his gal goes to the motel and I ain't real sure whut fer. All I knowed was here I was with Ida Sue, and she had the same look in her eyes as I had when I saw them sausage and aigs and waffles.

"Where you from, Clem?" she asks and sidles up real close.

"I'm from Hogwaller," I manages to git out. "Have you heard of hit?"

Wal, she jist chuckles a little and tells me about this ole hill boy that she dated once from Pine Bluff.

"Dumber than a load of dirt," she says, "But he knew whut a gal needs."

Wal, I warn't sure whut that is so I jist played ignerant.

"Want to hear a joke?" she asks, and I says I don't know many jokes but go ahead anyways.

"A hillbilly from Arkansas is driving on I-40 in his pickup truck when an Arkansas State Trooper pulls him over. He walks up to the driver, pulls out his notepad, looks at the driver and says, 'Got any I.

D.?' The hillbilly looks all bumfuzzled and says, 'Bout whut?'"

Wal, she breaks into a big laugh and I don't gits hit a'tall. She gits all mad and says I don't have a sense of humor and walks off in a huff. That was my first romantical doing and hit didn't turn out so good. I still don't know whut I did wrong, but wimmen is strange creetures, and I will jist have to figger them out as I go.

The bad thang was that I was shut out of my room and hit were two o'clock in the morning afore I could git into my bed. When Claypool woke me at 5:00 A.M. and asked if I wanted to go git some waffles, I throwed a shoe at him and went back to sleep. That was my first go around with wimmen, and hit didn't git any better any thing soon after that. Wal, I need to sign off. I'll tell you about my first real girlfriend in my next letter.

Yores til the aigs well done,

Clem

Clem's First Love

June 26, 2002

Dear Miss Amelia,

I left the Chef out of yore name because hit makes it seem a mite more friendly without hit. I hope you don't mind. If hit's a title that yore partial to, I will put Chef back in.

Wal, everythang's blooming all over the holler here. Hit's a little hot and hit jist makes me want to set around on the porch and whittle, but I knows I has to git back to work. The saw mill is shore a hard job but I'm putting a little money away each payday and hit all adds up. I hope yore doing good. I'se been trying to find sum reading on yore Designin' Wimmen group, but I ain't having much luck. Mebbe you'uns could see yore way clear to mail me some of yore pamplets. I would preciate hit so much.

Miss Amelia, in my last letter to you, I tolt you about my first bad go around on a date with a woman. Now I'se a'gonna tell you about my first real gal friend. Her name is Emma Jean Watson. She was the purtiest thang I had ever seed. I met her at a barn dance in Hootin' Holler one Satidday night and my life warn't the same after that. She had long brown hair, a tiny little nose, all her teeth, which was showed when she smiled a smile as wide as a barn door at me and asked me iffen I wanted to dance. My face turnt red and I couldn't do nothing but stare at my feet and stammer, so's she grabs my hand and pulls me out on the dance floor. Fer the next hour we danced, and I knows I didn't step on her feet once because mine were off the floor. I floated on air the rest of the night. When I got home, I could still see that purty face, and I recollected every freckle on her nose. But with ever true first love thar has to be some mudholes, and Emma Jean's paw was mine. You see he's the mayor of Hogwaller and has the biggest house in these hills. Even Claypool Pennywell hain't got the money this man has. He got so big in the lumber bissness that he bought up most of Hogwaller and purty much became mayor without an election. Even the boards in Ma and Pa's house came from Watson's Lumber Mill like most houses in the holler.

Emma Jean and me were hitting hit off purty good until the night she took me home to meet her maw and paw. Now this were about thirteen years ago and I was jist a country bumpkin. I has a little more upbranging now but then I was shy, and clumbsy, and didn't have much social larning likes I do now. Wal, hit started off bad and got worser as the evening went on. Afore I had left home that night, Maw had arned my best suit and made me scrub my body real good down at the sprang. She had give me some lilac water and I was smelling and looking right sassy. I has to admit I cleans up real good. I arrived at the Watson's house and rings the bell. Some man answers the door named Butler. He has on this real fine outfit. He looked better'n me if you can believe hit. I don't thank he was a fambly member though. I goes in and Butler says Mr. Watson will be right in, and I goes into this big parlor and sets down in a chair that would hold Pudge Wilson, the biggest man in Hogwaller.

Pudge always won the eating contests at the county fairs. Hit warn't really quite fair to everybody else considering that Pudge had to be weighed on the large butcher's scales at the stockyards. The only man who ever came close was Mr. Tate's boy Gurgy, but he jist didn't have the stumach that Pudge had. Anyhows, I'm a'sitting in the parlor and Mr. Watson comes into the room. He looks at me real hard and suddenly the chair gits even bigger, and I can feel myself shrinking into hit. He was nearly as big as Pudge, but a tad more solid and a whole heap nicer dressed. I was a'stammerin' and a'shufflin' my feet and trying to answer his questions when Emma Jean came down the stairs and rescued me. She took my hand in hern and led me into the dining room with her paw close behind, smoking a large cigar and waiting for me to make a wrong move, I am shore.

Wal, iffen I had been uneasy up to that point, it got worser in a hurry. We sits down at a table that were so long it wouldn't have fit into Maw and Paw's house. There were all manners of glasses and plates and knifes and sich. Thar musta' been at least four forks by my plate. They had a serving gal who brung us some greens in a bowl. They called it a sallet and everybody seemed right fond of hit. I warn't sure what to do because it was the kind of vittles we give to the hawgs. Thar was carrots and lettuce and maters plus some thangs I couldn't tell whut they were. But I was game and I picked up one of them forks, but I noticed Emma Jean pointing to one of the tothers, so's I picks hit up instead.

Wal, the whole time I'm a'tryin' to eat, I keep gitting all these questions from Emma Jean's maw and paw about my grades in school, what my prospects are, what my fambly's like, where do I live, what do my maw and paw do. I was feeling like one of them groundhogs that's been backed into a corner with no way out and the hounds closing in for the kill. By the time the meal was over and I had made a hunnerd more mistakes, I had came to realize somethang. I thank hit was the first time I knowed there was anuther world outside of Hogwaller and I didn't belong in hit. Emma Jean and I seed each other a few more times, but she knowed like me that I couldn't live in her world. I jist warn't ready. We was two of them star-crossed lovers like Romeo and Juliet in that play that Shakeaspear writ. I liked Emma Jean but I warn't going to die fer her. But Emma Jean was nice in her own way. She never made fun of me or made me feel like I warn't good enuff. That was to come later with Delilah Poindexter, but that's fer the next letter. I hope my romantical tales ain't boring you but you asked fer hit. Maw's got some milk she wants me to churn, so's I better git to hit. Thar's nothing better'n a cold glass of buttermilk on a hot day. And that butter on a piece of hot cornpone is nigh as close to heaven as a feller can git. Until next time I remain yore dutiful servant.

Yores until the butter flies,

Clem

Hogwallow's First Election

July 4, 2002

Dear Miss Amelia,

I knows I'm not a'givin' you much time to answer my letters but thangs are a'poppin' here in Hogwaller, hit being July 4 and all. I was a'goin' to tell you about Delilah Poindexter in this here letter, but too much is a'happening all at once, so's I'll have to git to her later.

You remember the Sims boy Celeriac who really isn't Celeriac a'tall but Cecil who married the Tucker gal after her daddy nearly kilt him with a shotgun and they had to git married, but the preacher had a corona so's they had to git another preacher to marry them? Wal, he's a'runnin' for mayor of Hogwaller, and you remembers me telling you about Emma Jean Watson in my last letter who I courted sum years ago and her daddy owns the sawmill and they have a servant named Butler and Mr. Watson didn't take kindly to me because his fambly is better'n mine? I thank you can see whut I am a'gittin' at. They's going to be an election in Hogwaller. I can't remember the last time we had a election. Folks around here jist kinda appoint theirselves to be thangs. Like Mr. Watson jist purty much appointed hisself mayor. It seems nobody else wanted the job.

Wal, now Cecil has flung his cap into the ring. He's a git-after-hit type of feller, having all that book larning at the technical school and all. Now I ain't too fond of Cecil cause he thanks we'uns in the Clodhopper household is ignerant. But he does have a good head on his shoulders, thanks to me for not using hit in my possum stew, and I thank he would make a good mayor. On the tother hand, you have Melville T. Watson, who has been mayor fer as long as anyone can remember and who is the paw to Emma Jean Watson who was my gal friend years ago which puts me betwixt a rock and a boulder, don't you know. The campainin' has already begun and the name calling and mud slinging is really flying.

You remember Jake the postman who got likkered up and fell

asleep and froze his toes which had to be chopped off because they was frostbit 'cepting for the big toe which caused him some discomfort until you gals sent him a gadget to chop off the nail? Wal, he's a'limpin' a little more than usual since he is a'carryin' all this campaign mail around the holler, and don't you know the Sears catalogue would come out at the same time as when the election is heatin' up? Pore ol' Jake is a'sweatin' like a plow mule that's been worked hard and put up wet. He's either a'freezing' and losing his toes or a'sweatin' and having a corona. Anyways, hit's hot all over here and the election ain't the half of hit.

Here's whut really grinds my axe. The guv'ment has sent out letters that they is going to be a'cuttin' welfare checks. It seems the economy is lower than Shanky Branch Crik in the summer, and money is tighter than Pappy's long johns after they's been warshed. All of Hogwaller is up in arms about hit, and they's risen as a community and gotten a petition to send to Warshington. All 102 residents of legal age in Hogwaller has signed hit. Them that can't write jist put an X, so's they was at least accounted fer. Of course Cecil and Melville T. has both started politicking about how's they will go to Warshington and talk to the President. Paw says you can't trust no politician as fur as you can throw him. They's all liars and thiefs. He thanks Arkansaw should jist secede from the union and start their own guv'ment. He thanks that Mr. Clinton could come back and run the place and they'd be a chicken in ever pot. He can't figger out why Mr. Clinton couldn't uv been President fer life. Wal, he could be President of Arkansaw or maybe dictator if we secede. Paw don't keer as long as they don't fool with his welfare check. Why, they could even send that Monica girl along with him. The folks in Hogwaller never could figger out whut all the fuss was about that woman. So's Mr. Clinton lied a little, and played around a little on his wife. Hereabouts them is jist social fox paws and no reason to git so het up about.

Anyways, Maw has looked into chopping out some expenses so's they can git from month to month. She has suggested that Paw git a job, but any job he could git around here would pay less than the welfare check, so Paw ain't biting on that one. Paw has suggested that Maw quit her snuff, but I thank Paw had better let that one alone. Until Maw has had her coffee and snuff in the morning, she's touchier than an ole she bear. I'm jist avoiding both of them until everythang gits back to normal.

Hit's for shore that this is the most activity I have seed in these hills in sum years. I'm a'goin' to find a big shade tree, git some of Maw's good lemonade, and whittle my trubbles away. I ain't no politician but I ain't no fool nuther.When life throws lemons at yore head, make some juice out of hit and find a good shade tree. Stay cool whar you air and iffen you want to holp us out in Warshington, git them Designin' Wimmen to whip up a gadget whut will tell when a politician is a'lyin'. Paw says you know a politician is a'lyin' iffen his mouth is open, but I thank some gadget would be right helpful iffen you kin do hit. I'm goin' to git this letter ready for Jake, so I'll back on out of here.

Yores till the lemon drops,

Clem

The Mudslinging Begins

July 7, 2002

Dear Miss Chef Amelia,

I added Chef back to yore name because I has a cooking question that I hopes you can answer fer me. I hopes we has more luck with this'un than we did with the possum. You remembers the possum whut I writ you about in my first letter whut was road kill and was torn up so bad and we'uns asked you about fer a recipe and wound up puttin' hit in a stew? Me and Paw was a'sittin' by the riverbank the tother day and Paw spied one of them green looking ducks a'swimmin' on the water. Wal, Paw never goes anywheres without his trusty rifle, so he levels down on the critter and pops him a good'un. We takes food wherevers we finds hit. He sikked ol' Buford to go and git hit. Buford is our dog, don't you know. Buford is one of them 57 various dogs, but he has good huntin' instinks, so's he jumps into that river and swims out there and brangs hit back to us.

We took hit home to Maw fer supper. Now, we's tried duck afore, and hit didn't taste all that good. The first'un that we cooked was as green in hit's innards as hit was in hit's outtards. Maw put hit into some flour and throwed hit into a skillet in some lard as usual, but this thang was awful even by Hogwaller standards. Maw looked a little green her own self when we brang this'un to her. So's she's asking me to ask you if there hain't some recipe fer duck that can make hit taste proper. She saw a recipe once fer somethang named duck on a orange. Do you know whut that is and do you have a recipe fer hit? Iffen you do, we'uns would be right glad to git hit.

Speaking of ducks and hunting and sich, I'm trying to stay low during this election season. You remember whut I was a'tellin' you about in my last letter where the Sims boy that we thought was Celeriac but is really Cecil is a'runnin' for mayor against Melville T. Watson who owns the lumber mill and is the Daddy to Emma Jean Watson whut I was a'squirin' fer a time when I was jist a young man? Hit seems folks is a'takin' sides in a big way. I ain't seed this much excitement since one of our own was in that White House in Warshington. Hit seems that Melville T. is using his money to buy votes. I know hit's a bad thang, but he's a'throwin' money like water on a far. Now Cecil don't have the means to win that-a-way. So's he's spreading lies about how Emma Jean Watson is a'sleepin' with ever man in Hogwaller to git her daddy votes. Cecil wants to besmirch the Watson name and git votes that-a-way. Wal, hit's got folks all stirred up and turnt fambly members aginst fambly members. Hit's made me right mad because I know Emma Jean would never do sich a thang. She was my first true love and I known better than to believe sich lies. So's I don't like Cecil fer a'doin that, but I don't thank Melville T. should be buying votes nuther. I may jist do one of them write in thangs and put Paw's name into the pot. He's got some good idees on how to improve thangs here in the holler. He's even come up with an idee for a two seater outhouse jist in case Ma Nature calls more than one person at the same time. I thank I would jist have to hold hit if Paw were in thar. A good spark would blow up the whole outhouse, and I don't want to die in sich a way. I've heard of people buying natural gas for stoves and sich. Paw could keep us supplied fer years and hit's free.

Anyways, that's jist one idee. We also has a water problem here in the holler. Shanky Branch Crik supplies the dranking water fer most of the folks here. Well, thar's the Poindexter fambly who has the Delilah gal whut I will be a'tellin' you about later who ruint my life in a romantical way who lives close to the head of the crik and their house is built over the crik. Burl, the head of the clan, built his house right over the crik and cut a hole in the floor. During the winter, he don't even bother to go to the outhouse, iffen you gits my drift. Now, that can't be good fer the dranking water, so Paw's working on digging a well fer Maw, and he figgers he could form sum group to dig wells fer all the famblies in Hogwaller. Paw's always figgerin' on thangs to help people, so I thank he would be a good mayor. I'm going to git the word around about whut I plan to do with them write in votes. Paw jist might git enuff to win whut with Cecil a'lyin' to git votes and Melville T. a'tryin' to buy them. I'll let you know how hit's a'goin'. I hope yore well. Send me that duck on a orange recipe if you has hit.

A duckin' and a'dodgin'

Clem

Amelia's Recipe for Duck

July 15, 2002

Dear Clem,

I have a solution to your duck problem. I hope you have not skinned this fine bird yet because the meat can be quite delicate. Please leave the skin on and write to me at the first opportunity. The duck must still have the skin on in order to taste the fine flavors of the bird. Should the bird look as green as the last one, I am guessing that it is what is known as a teal. This may not be suitable for consumption.

You will need the following ingredients:

Orange marmalade (or orange jam)
½ pint of strong spirits
(I usually recommend Grand Marnier, but the local liquer in your area will do)
Salt and pepper to taste
1 slab of fine bacon
Orange zest to taste

I am sorry that I cannot give you further instructions as of yet, but it is of most importance to find out how you have managed the duck.

Fondly,

Chef Amelia Winslow Blythe

Clem and Delilah

July 23, 2002

Dear Miss Chef Amelia,

Thank you for writing back so soon on how to cook a duck because this thang has Ma plumb flustered. To answer yore question, no, we have not skint the duck yit. Ma makes a pot of biling water and souses the duck down into hit and plucks the feathers, but she leaves the skin alone. We hain't shore iffen hit is a teal duck or not. Paw says he don't name the critters; he jist shoots them. You said fer the recipe to include some orange jam, which we got, and salt and pepper, which we got, strong liquor, which is more plentiful around here than anythang, and a slab of bacon.

Wal, I kin tell you now, iffen we had that big slab of bacon, Maw would jist throw this duck away and cook hit. I am not shore whut you mean by managing the duck. I can't manage hit a'tall. Hit's daid. Ma hain't managing too good nuther. I jist heard her tell Paw to give hit to the dogs cause by the time we gits hit cooked hit will be spiled anyways. I'm sorry if I have wasted yore time, but I thank you will forgive me when I tell you about Delilah Poindexter.

You remember I tolt you about the Poindexter fambly whut Delilah belongs to who is the girl who turnt me aginst wimmen and whose daddy is Burl Poindexter who lives at the head of Shanky Branch Crik and who built his house over the crik and cut a hole in the floor so's he wouldn't have to go to the outhouse in the winter? Wal, you'd have to go way beyond Hogwaller and Hootin' Holler to find a sorrier man than ole Burl Poindexter. He's a rogue and scoundrel and them is his good points. The only purty thang about the Poindexter fambly is Delilah and her purtiness is on the outside cause she has a heart as cold as an Arkansaw winter in these hills. I don't know who she got her looks after, but she got that cold heart from her paw. A meaner and more spiteful man can't be fount in these hollers. You may be gitting the idee I don't like him and you'd be right.

Wal, gitting on with the story, I started sparking Delilah when I was eighteen. She was nineteen and an older woman, don't you know. Of course, she were a heap more worldly than me, so's I was in over my head from the git go. Like her namesake in the Bible, she was a designin' woman. She weaved a spell over me and I couldn't see past them good looks, so I fell victim to her and her fambly.

Here's how the story goes. Paw owned all the land from jist below our house all the way up to the head of Shanky Branch Crik. It were a prime piece of real estate. Ole Burl and his fambly wanted to move into the holler and he had his eye on Paw's land at the head of the crik. Paw didn't want to sell, but Burl offered him in trade a patch of land that he owned a couple of miles up in the holler. Hit's nothing but scrub brush and briars and has a smell that would make Paw's natural gas seem like eau de colonie. Nothing but snakes and jackrabbits could live thar. So natural, Paw told him no. Wal, Burl ain't one to take no fer an answer, so he turned to the biggest ace he had in the hole and that were Delilah.

Delilah started coming by the house reg'lar, branging things to Maw and Paw, like aigs and taters and sich, pretending to be all neighborly, but she was a'doing thangs to me with her eyes and womanly wiles. We started hittin' hit off, and the next thang I knowed me and Delilah were the talk of Hogwaller. Ole Burl stayed in the shadows and moved us around like checker pieces until Delilah convinced me we should git hitched. I agreed and we set the date and started making plans.

Then Burl comes to Pa and says hit would be a great gesture on Pa's part iffen he were to deed that land over to the newlywed couple as a wedding gift. After all, I were a'gittin' the purtiest gal in Hogwaller, and she deserved a nice place to live. Paw has a heart of gold, don't you know, and he agreed to give up the land to me and Delilah to build our house. Burl agreed to build the house as his gift to us, but he had to have the property in his name to git money from the bank for lumber. So's Paw deeds hit over to him and Burl starts on the house.

Everthang is rolling along and the house is going to be finished about the time the wedding vows is going to be spoke. Now comes the hard part fer me. The next thang I knows Delilah leaves town with a drummer feller who has been a'wooin' her unbeknownst to everyone cepting the Poindexter fambly. They takes off to Pine Bluff and I never sees her again. My heart is broke, don't you know. Wal, Paw goes to Burl and asks fer his land back, and Burl says no that hit is a binding contract, and he almost has the house done so hit's now his property. He says that Delilah is of age and kin make up her own mind who she wants to git hitched to. Paw wants to settle hit with his 12 gauge, but Maw steps in afore it gits to that point. Burl offers Paw the scrub brush land as a token of no hard feelings, but Paw has plenty of hard feelings. So, there I were with no land, no house, and no bride. I slunk out of the holler and went to stay with my Cousin Homer until thangs died down a mite, and I could come back with a tad of dignity. Paw lost the nicest piece of land in the holler and wound up with a few acres of rocks and scrub brush. Paw thanks some good mite come out of the land. Hit's kinda marshy, so Paw thanks hit mite be a good place to drill fer water. He hates to thank whut mite be in Shanky Branch iffen it came out of Ole Burl.

Anyways, You can see why hit gnaws at me now. I was jist a tool fer Delilah to use to git her paw whut he wanted. You sees now why I don't like to talk about hit and why I have turnt aginst wimmen. Paw is determined to git even with the Poindexters some day. Knowing Paw, iffen I was Ole Burl, I'd stay close to home for a mite. Accidents do happen in the woods around here, iffen you know whut I mean. I do preciate yore kindness to me. Hit has restored some of my faith in wimmen. Is the woodpeckers still working on yore house? Iffen I can bottle up some of Paw's natural gas, I'll send hit to you. Hit will git shed of anythang. Hit's a moneymaker iffen I can figger out how to do hit. I reckon I'll git on out of here.

Yores til the outhouse flies,

Clem

A "Who Done It?"

July 27, 2002

Dear Miss Amelia

Wal, I'll jist tell you hit's like one of them soap oprys around here. You remembers me in my last letter telling you about Delilah Poindexter who was my intended financee who jilted me at the altar for a traveling salesman and I never seed her agin and her paw Burl Poindexter who hornswaggled Paw out of the best piece of prime real estate in Hogwaller and who is running fer mayor aginst Cecil who we thought was Celeriac but twernt at all and they's both been using foul means to git elected and has folks a'feudin' at each other all over the holler? Hit jist keeps gitting worser and worser.

You remembers Annabelle Tucker who Cecil was sneaking out and sparking with until old man Tucker fount out about hit and he took a shotgun to kill Cecil but wound up making Cecil and Annabelle git hitched, but Brother Johnson the preacher had a corona and Brother Billings had to take his place? Wal, it seems that Annabelle was a'givin' one of them campaign speeches for Cecil and somebody from the crowd chucked a rotten tomater at her and spoilt the speech and her Sunday go-to-meeting dress to boot. Some people in the crowd said hit was one of Burl Poindexter's sons but nobody knows which a one hit was. Burl has nine boys and all of them are at home, so's hit's a crap shoot as to which of them boys coulda done hit. There's Merle, Darryl, Farrel, Harold, Clovis, Clavelle, Clancy, Clayton, and Jethro. They's purty much all like Burl and the whole fambly is pulling hard for Melville T. Watson in the mayor's election. Ole Burl has so many offsprang that they could pert near elect Melville T. by theirselves.

Now Cecil is hopping mad because his bride of less than a year is a'cryin' and demanding that something be done. Cecil is saying that if hit's dirty politics that Melville T. wants, that's whut he'll git. My plan to git Paw elected by write in votes in going nicely, and he may be the onliest one left standing by the time the election is over. But the soap opry hain't over. Now git this. A man never knows whut the next day is a'gonna brang and hit's always calmest afore the storm. I thank you know whut I'm a'gittin' at. Yep, Delilah Poindexter has come back to Hogwaller and she has a young'un with her. Hit seems that she married the drummer man that whisked her away on our wedding day and they had a baby. Wal, he was a no account and he left Delilah and the baby and jist disappeared. Delilah went out on her own fer a while, but she jist couldn't make hit on her own outside Hogwaller, so's she come back to the holler with a little girl to add to the Poindexter clan. I hain't seed her yit, but folks down at the mercantile have tolt me she's been askin' bout me and whut I'm a'doin'. Burl has welcomed her back with open arms. Now he has somebody to fix his meals and clean up around the house which is like a pig sty whut with all them boys around. Kin you imagine cooking and cleaning for nine brothers and her paw with a child to take keer of? Now, I ain't the smartest of the Clodhopper fambly, but I kin tell you this. She kin look at me with them big brown cow eyes and dress real slinky and parade around, but I ain't going over that road agin. Fool me once, shame on you, fool me twict, shame on me.

Paw has been gone into the lowlands all day to git supplies for some canning Maw is a'goin' to do. She's got all kinds of vegetables she has growed and has been paring away all day gitting them ready to be cooked and canned. I worry about Paw when he goes into town because he is too good hearted and folks takes advantage of him. Paw will drank a mite more when he's away from Maw and he sometimes forgits what he's gone to town after. Maw tolt him to git some sugar, salt, vinegar, flour, meal, and a good supply of Mason jars. I hope he makes hit back with all them items. Maw is cantankerous around canning time. I stay as fer away as possible when she's in one of her snits.

I've been doing some sprang cleaning in my own little shack. My house is about a mile away and jist fer enough that Maw can't pop over ever day and shoot the breeze or git me to do chores or run errands fer her. She still thanks of me as a small boy instead of a growed man who has thangs of his own to do. Besides, Paw has already tolt me to find a likely site to drill for water on his scrub patch he got from Burl. Burl don't know hit, but Paw has something in the works fer him. Like I tolt you, Paw has a heart of gold but he don't forgit when somebody's done him wrong.

Paw was a'talking to Melville T. the tother day about Burl spiling the water at the head of the sprang, but Melville T. don't want to make his biggest supporter mad, so's he jist tells Paw he can't do nothing. Paw comes home madder'n a wet cat and says he needs to git to work on his surprise fer Burl. I hope this ain't become one of them abcesses fer Paw. Anyways, you can see whut I mean about the going's on around here seeming like a soap opry. I'll write agin' when I got more news.

I hope I ain't a'boring you with my life.

Yore good friend,

Clem

Amelia Wields Her Influence

My Dear Clem,

What an exciting life you lead! It makes my life seem rather drab and dull, which I suppose it is since all I do is work. Pursuing a career leaves little time for interaction with others in a social way. Though your romantic interlude with Delilah left you stranded at the altar, at least you had a romantic interlude. I suppose there have been many suitors that I could have had, but I was too busy with my career. I do hope that you will be able to love again, but please do not make the mistake of going back to that woman. She will just break your heart and further poison your mind to all women.

I am just incensed at what Burl Poindexter has done to your family and to Shanky Branch Creek! First of all, it is obvious that he is a reprobate and total scoundrel to use such cunning and conniving means to obtain the land your father prized so highly. If he were in New York, we would have him in court suing for breach of contract or abandonment or some other technicality. I know things there in Hogwallow are not settled that way and your method is probably best. I did write to the McDonald's headquarters for you regarding their hiring practices at the McDonald's there in your area, but I do not expect anything substantial to happen. I'm glad you have the job at the lumber mill in the interim.

The Poindexter family building their house over Shanky Branch Creek is another matter. This must indeed be looked into. Fecal matter in a water source for a community is nothing to take lightly. All manner of disease-carrying bacteria can be transmitted this way. I will inform the EPA immediately. I recently had occasion to call the EPA, so they know who I am and what influence I carry. A very callous fellow was cutting trees close to my property and leaving it open to all manner of erosion. He was loud and abusive but I stood my ground. I called the EPA and they came out and saw what damage he was doing and fined him ten thousand dollars and hit him with sanctions that will prevent future problems. He never knew that it was I who had informed on him, which I think I will just leave that way. I believe him to be a very vindictive man, and, after all, I am just a poor, defenseless woman. But that conflict was so exhilarating! I can see why the election is such a big issue and why the community is so stirred up. Conflict heightens the senses and evokes emotions that I never dreamed I had. It makes me want to come to Hogwallow and be a participant in the activities there. Oh, well. Back to my humdrum life. I will keep you informed about what the EPA plans to do. Some representative may call on you to hear your story. Good luck and keep me informed on Delilah and the election and all the other interesting conflicts coming out of your little community.

Your friend and confidante,

Amelia

Ma Has Her Hair Done

August 12, 2002

Dear Miss Amelia,

It was shore nice to hear from you You have become a real pen-pal to me. I'm a'doin' all my letter writin' now, and Maw is not helping me a'tall. She thanks I may be sweet on you since I hain't asking her to write fer me. I want to thank you fer yore good idees about Burl and our water problem, but I don't reckon the EPA folks will come back here into Hogwaller to fix our problems. We's jist poor hill famblies and them guv'ment folk don't have time fer us.

Here's some news you might like, being a woman and all. Maw got hit into her head that mebbe changing her hair might make her more looksome to Paw. Maw tolt me she writ to you about Paw not paying her no mind in the bedroom, if you know whut I mean. Now, I ain't one to discuss the bedroom with a woman I ain't never seed, and it makes me feel a little queer to even mention hit, but I know thar's some problems so I will jist leave hit at that. Anyhow, Maw thanks that Paw would pay more attention to her iffen she did something more stylish with her hair, so she scoots off to the lowlands to git styled. Now keep in mind that Maw hain't never had anyone else to touch her hair, so's this was a mite worrisome to her.

Wal, she goes into a hair saloon called Curl Up and Dye, and this big ole gal tells her to have a seat and someone would be with her soon. Maw kinda looks the place over, and she's gitting nervouser and nervouser. One woman has this big metal hood over her head and hit's making all sorts of noise. Another one looks like she's got some sheet metal in her hair, and hit's jist rolled up all over her head. Maw said hit hurt her ears with all them machines going and all them wimmen talking at the same time. She was glad when finally one of them saloon ladies tolt her to sit in one of them big cheers. This lady starts to fixing Maw's hair. She washes hit, which Maw kinda liked being fussed over thataway. Then she uses this machine to dry hit. Then she applies all kinds of liquids from these bottles on a shelf. Then she rolls hit up so tight that Maw thanks hits being pulled out by the roots. After all this, they put one of them helmet machines over Maw's head. Now Maw ain't real keen with thangs being put over her head, so she complains a mite but the lady tells her that everythang will be alright and for Maw to relax.

Wal, Maw relaxes so much that she jist drifts right off to sleep. The next thang she knows the lady is telling her that she is done and Maw kin go home. Now Paw don't know what Maw has been doing all day so when she gits home hit's past suppertime and Paw is fit to be tied. Paw don't notice much, but when Maw took off her Sunday hat, hit nearly sent Paw into a spasm. Hit were bright orangy in color and in little ringlets all over her head. First Paw were so shocked that he couldn't say nuthing. Then he started in to laughing. He jist nearly got down on the floor and rolled around. Now this twernt the reaction that Maw had expected and the next thang Paw knowed, a skillet were heading for his noggin. Paw beat a hasty retreat and went over to the Simses until Maw simmered down.

But that ain't the worstest part. All them chemicals the saloon ladies had used on Maw's hair had caused some sort of problem. Them little curls jist started breaking off like they's chalk. Maw jist set down and cried. Paw was feeling bad about laughing at Maw, and he tolt her that the next day he would drive her into town and have the saloon ladies to try and fix hit. The next day Paw did jist that. Them ladies was jist as sorry as they could be. They tolt Maw that it was the lady's first time whut had done her hair and she would be farred. Now Maw didn't want to git the lady in trouble. She jist wanted her hair fixed. They did the best they could, but hit was going to be a long time afore Maw would be able to show her hair agin.

So come next Sunday meeting, Maw wore a bright scarf around her head and put on some dangly earrangs. She took the biggest, floppiest hat she had and put hit on her head. She were a sight! Doggone iffen she warn't the talk of the ladies of the congregation. You could see them during the sermon sneaking peeks at Maw, and after church they met in little groups and whispered amongst theirselves something fierce. Maw was jist in tears and so ashamed that she didn't wait fer Paw, but jist walked home and went to bed.

When next Sunday rolled around, Maw didn't want to go to church. Now, you have to understand that Maw hain't missed a Sunday preaching in nigh on to forty years. But she put on her scarf, her hat, and finest Sunday outfit and said that she didn't keer iffen they laughed or not, she would not miss church for some hens a'cluckin'. Howsomeever, she did not sit in her reg'lar pew in the front, hoping she would be noticed less in one of them back seats. Wal, folks started to arrive and don't you know the queerest thang happened. As the ladies trooped into church, every one of them was a'wearin' a bright scarf and a big hat! Maw couldn't believe her eyes. The church ladies had liked how she looked so much that they were a'wearin' the same thang. Maw had started one of them fads in Hogwaller.

Wal, the upshot of hit all was that Maw moved up several notches on the social ladder here in the holler, and she has been invited to several shindigs whut the wimmen's circle holds each month to speak about clothing styles. Her hair is growing out fine. Thangs worked out alright enuff, but she hain't going back to no saloon. Life's jist that way iffen you thank about hit. When you git hit in the face, you can jist set down and cry, or you kin git up and make the best of hit and see whut happens. Maw is a gitter-upper and don't thank Paw hain't noticed. He's right proud of her and tolt her so. I thank thangs in the bedroom might be better now. Since I'm a'talking about church, hit reminds me of an incident last Sunday whut took place in church and has caused more problems fer Hogwaller. It seems politics has entered the church. I want to tell you about whut happened, but I'll have to save hit for the next letter.

Yores till the hair styles,

Clem

A Fight in the Church

August 16, 2002

Dear Miss Amelia,

When I left you last time I tolt you I would make this here letter about politics and the church. I kin write about this first hand because I saw hit at work right here in Hogwaller. Maw always tolt me never to mix politics and religion. She also tolt me never to argue with fools. Wal, this election has brung fools out of every outhouse in Hogwaller and they's mixing politics and religion something fearful. Hit happened three weeks ago on a Sunday in our church. Our church is the First Footwashing Baptist Church of the Second Coming of Hogwaller. We is purty traditional in our ways and don't take much truck with folks who like to change the Bible to suit their own needs. Of course, Maw and Paw have been members for nigh 40 years and have been faithful in their attendance. I goes every now and then, and I happened to hit jist the one that I'm a'goin' to tell you about.

Wal, it started out simple enough. You remembers how I tolt you in my last letter that Maw had her hair done and the saloon ladies at the Curl Up and Dye had messed hit up somethang turrible and hit had gotten brittle and fell out and Maw covered hit up with a scarf and hat and all the church ladies started to a'wearin' the same thang because they thought hit were high fashion? They's all wearing their scarfs and biggest bonnets this Sunday and the church were full. Everybody seemed to know that there was something a'brewin', and they didn't want to miss hit. Even the Poindexter clan was there. There was Burl, Merle, Darryl, Farrel, Harold, Clovis, Clavelle, Clancy, Clayton, Jethro, and Delilah and her baby girl. I have to say that Delilah was a'lookin' right fetching in that Sunday go-to-meeting dress she had on. It seemed to be filled out in all the right places, if you know whut I mean. Now, like I said, I hain't going down that road agin, but that don't mean a man can't preciate what Ma Nature has done in the female form.

Now, where was I? Wal, Brother Johnson started with the

announcements. Becky Sawyer's prize coon hound had nine pups a week ago and she'd be a'lookin' to give them away in a few weeks, and I could see all the coonhunters perk up their ears. Old Miss Cartwright fell coming out of the outhouse and rolled down the hill and skint herself up a mite. Her hip is twinging a bit, and she could use some help with the warshing fer a spell til hit's better. Opal Stone kilt her first deer and carried hit home by herself. Now Opal may be a girl, but she's a dead shot and near as strong as ary boy. And it seems that the Turners has a young'un with the colic, so iffen someone wanted to take the fambly some vittles to help Missus Turner out, hit would be preciated.

After the announcements was over, you could see that Brother Johnson was excited by all the crowd that had showed up. The Poindexter clan was there, Melville T. Watson and his fambly were there, including Emma Jean who were my first love as I tolt you in another letter, and Cecil, who we thought was celeriac but twernt at all, and his wife Annabelle were there. Something were a'brewin' as you can see. Wal, Brother Johnson started in to preaching, and he was a'layin' down some gospel. The tuh-huttins were a'flyin' every whichaway and the sermon were about gitting along with each other in the church regardless of yore religion or skin color or fambly and that we was all equal in the eyes of God. I guess Ole Burl must of had some shine afore he arrived because he were a'gittin' the message and "Amenning" every word out of the preacher's mouth. Delilah looked a mite flushed and moved down the pew a tad and hunkered down in her seat.

The sermon were almost over and Brother Johnson had worked the congregation into a fever pitch. It even had me pert nigh ready to answer the call, but I stood my ground. Brother Johnson is calling fer sinners to come forward and repent of their evil deeds, to renounce Satan, and to confess their sins to the church and renew their souls. All of a sudden, Clovis Poindexter jumps to his feet with a wild look in his eyes and starts a'hollerin', "I did hit! I did hit! I chucked that rotten termater at Annabelle and spoilt her Sunday go-to-meeting dress. Melville T. tolt me to do hit. I'se guilty as sin, Preacher." Wal, Annabelle jist bursts into tears and Cecil, seeing her all teary again, comes a'flyin' across the pews to git to Clovis. He falls into the whole clan with arms and legs jist a' flailin'.

Now the whole congregation is in an uproar. Wimmen are crying

63

and running every which a way. Some men are a'fightin' and some are a'tryin' to break hit up, and Brother Johnson is asking for peace in God's house, but nobody were a'hearin' him. When a hymn book went a'flyin' by his head, he took that as a sign from God and hunkered down by the baptismal. Now whilst all this is a'goin' on, I grabs Maw and Delilah and the baby and heads outside. Hit's jist my nature to pertect wimmen and children when I can. In a while, Paw comes out leading Cecil who looks all frazzled with his suit all tore and knots and bruises all about his head. I could of tolt him that if you fights one Poindexter, you has to fight 'em all.

After things settle down a mite, Brother Johnson asks everyone to come back into the church. Melville T. and his fambly and the Poindexters are gone home, and Cecil starts in to lectioneering about how we kin see now how dirty politics has entered Hogwaller and to elect him on election day. Brother Johnson says that the church ain't the place fer politics and how Cecil should go home and look at the skeletons in his own closet. So Cecil leaves all in a huff a'pulling Annabelle who is still crying and a'caterwallin'. Hit's a long time until November and a lot of thangs can happen twixt now and then. So, Miss Amelia, hit looks like my campain to elect Paw on a write in has jist gotten better. I may put up some of them flyers around the hills to let people know there is another choice. How's do I go about printing them flyers up? Iffen you could help with the wording, I would appreciate hit. I know yore busy with yore own problems, but write when you can.

Yore Hogwaller Friend,

Clem

Amelia's Church Story

August 24, 2002

Dear Clem,

My! How exciting it must be to live in a place like Hogwallow and see and experience all the scintillating events that occur each day. It seems so different from my hum-drum world. A fist fight in a church! I have never heard of such a thing. I am a Presbyterian and we would never think of resorting to physical violence to settle differences.

Why, just the other day, Maybelle Higgenbotham and Karen Van Goosenburg had a disagreement, and they simply expressed their feelings and left it at that. Now that is the way to resolve an argument. It seems that Maybelle wanted the chairs in the basement cafeteria arranged in a certain order, and Karen wanted them in another arrangement. Well, Maybelle is the chairwoman of the Committee on Chair Arranging, so she told Karen that it would have to be done her way since she is the leader of that committee. Karen fumed and stewed, but Maybelle had the last word and had the chairs arranged her way and everyone went home. Well, Karen has a key to the church, so unbeknown to everyone, she went to the church that night and rearranged the chairs like she wanted them.

The next day was Sunday and the day of the big luncheon at the church. Ironically, the sermon that day by Pastor Susan was on cooperation among church members. Yes, I know what you're thinking. We have a woman minister in our church. While that would be contrary to Baptist beliefs, we in the Presbyterian church think women can lead as well or better than men. Anyway, the congregation went into the cafeteria to have their lunch, and Maybelle could not believe her eyes. The chairs had been rearranged. Well, she approached Karen and gave her a severe tongue lashing and Karen left the church in tears. Now, that is the way to resolve differences in a civil manner in a proper church. No fights, no name calling, just severe admonishment and everyone is happy. You might try that in your church. Wouldn't that be so much better than fisticuffs? Karen will see the error of her ways and be a stronger member because she was put in her place.

Still, there may be more excitement in the Hogwallow way if that is what a person were looking for. I'm just so glad you did the noble thing and removed your mother and Delilah and her child from such rowdiness. You are such a gentleman. Yet, I know if the situation called for it, you would be like a colossus, a Hercules striding among mortals. A man among children, dropping that Poindexter clan like flies with a wave of your hand. Your muscles rippling and each sinew bursting with raw power as you brushed them aside like chaff in the wind. Striding among them your shirt torn all asunder and your golden skin glistening from exertion as you…My! My! I seem to have lost my train of thought. I almost have the vapors thinking about such violence. I must not let myself think of you in such a fashion. I do declare that sometimes I think that I have deviated from my upbringing with such thoughts that come into my head.

My dear Clem, I must come to Hogwallow in the near future. There is so much there that I could write about for my *Designing Women* magazine. The magazine will feature me in their next issue, and having such notoriety will allow me to call the shots when I approach the committee about making the trip. I could write off the trip as a business expense since I will be using the occasion to gather information for the magazine. I could research the different family recipes of the Hogwallow denizens and use that information to write an interesting article on Appalachian culinary skills. How interesting that would be, and I would, of course, stay with families in the area as I did my research and experience the ambiance of the area as well as the tasty "vittles" of the local families. Naturally, I would want to meet you and your family since we have become friends, albeit so far by correspondence through the mail. I feel as if I am part of the Clodhopper clan and would like to meet you face to face, so to speak. While I am there, I could look further into the water situation on the Poindexter place and give the EPA more information through my first hand experience. Of course, I would like to prepare a meal for your family and let them taste a more delicate fare that what they normally experience.

So the learning experience would be a two way street. I think your family will like me, though I am a Presbyterian. I know there are a lot of activities going on and you're very busy right now, but if there is a lull in the near future when I would be welcome in Hogwallow, please make me aware and I will plan accordingly. Until then, I will say adieu and wish you well.

Affectionately yours,

Amelia

Rufus and the Moonshine

September 1, 2002

Dear Miss Amelia,

Boy, Howdy! Hit's been busy around here. Ma's cleaning house and hit's pert nigh drove Paw crazy, even more than he usually is. Haw! Haw! When she gits in one of her cleaning moods, folks jist need to stay away, which I tries to do. Paw ain't so lucky. You hain't seen nothing so funny as Paw scrubbing them floors with a bucket and mop. Hit looks like he has the itch and don't know where to scratch. Water is being slung everywhere, and even the cat can't stand hit and heads for dryer ground. He'll work until Maw gits disgusted and takes a broom to his head and runs him out, which is whut he was a shootin' fer in the first place. Paw don't know why the house needs to be cleaned so often. With jist him and Maw there, he says they don't make much of a mess. He thanks he is neat as fur as men goes. Why he even takes a bath at least once a week, which he says is twict as much as most men in the holler. So he feels that Maw is purty lucky on the whole. Maw says that the place gets dirty even iffen they don't make hit that way. Paw says he can't understand doing some thangs like dusting. Hit jist comes back. Maw says the same thang about Paw. When she throws him out, he jist comes back. Wal, I knows they is jist a'jokin' with each other, and that makes it finer than snuff and not half as dusty. Anyhows, I ain't a'goin' over there until Maw is done.

Hit must be that time of year. Hit jist keeps gitting stranger and stranger around here. Rufus Sweeney passed by the house the tother day and he was carrying a load of sugar in his old pickup truck. Now folks in these parts knows Rufus, and them that do knows he ain't carrying that sugar home to make pies and jam. His wife is a large woman and she likes sweet thangs, but she couldn't cook up that much sugar in a month of Sundays. Rufus has been known to do a heap of moon shining in his time. He even spent a spell in the Big House when he were caught by the revenooers. But he's at hit agin and I won't be surprised to see some strangers with axes and guns riding through

68

Hogwaller looking fer his still.

Rufus says that a man can't make much of a living on the scrub land in these hills. He can't understand why the guv'ment would rather give him a welfare check than let him make shine and earn a honest living. He says hit ain't American. I thank Rufus could make a go of hit iffen he would quit dranking whut he made. But he likes to drank while he works and that ain't a good combination.

Rufus is purty smart about hiding his shine. I was a'sittin' in his house one day jist passing the time, gabbing about the weather and the election, when I started a'hearing these strange popping noises. Rufus didn't seem to be concerned, but hit got to bothering me, so's I asked him whut hit was. He laughed real big and walked over to a corner of the house and pried up a piece of the floor. He started to pull jars of shine out from under the house. He had put the jars of shine under the floor, and when they started to seal, they made a popping sound. I guess hit was lucky that them revenooers didn't stay long on their visits.

Them revenooers never woulda caught Rufus the first time iffen he had not made a mistake with one of his customers. Ever little community has hits town drunks. Hootin' Holler has Chub Taylor and we has Bernie Crawford, and hit would be a contest worth seeing to know which a one could drank more. Wal, Bernie got in a bad way needing a drink one night and he knowed that Rufus was a'going to make a run, so's he hides out near Rufus's house when he starts a'loadin' his truck to make the run. When Rufus is done, He throws some straw into the back and puts a tarp over the load and heads into the house to put the floor back into place. Whilst he's gone, Bernie crawls out of the bushes and starts to pull out a couple of jugs of shine when he hears Rufus coming out. He jumps into the back of the truck and lays low, hoping to jump out at the first chance without Rufus spotting him. Wal, Rufus is rolling along purty good and Bernie can't make a jump fer hit, so's he jist figgers he'll have a few swigs until he gits his chance. First thang you know, he's three sheets in the wind and ain't a'keerin' iffen he gits out or not. Rufus hits town and pulls in to the local saloon to make a drop and that's when hit happens. While Rufus is inside, the brakes on the truck gives out and hit starts a'rollin' backards. Now Bernie ain't so drunk that he don't realize the problem, so he drops the tailgate and bails out and the truck nearly runs over him, but fools and drunks is lucky that way. He don't git a scratch.

Howsomeever, the truck rolls back into the loading dock of the feed and grain store and them bottles come a'crashin' out and breaking, and shine starts flowing all over the street. Bernie says he ain't never seed such a waste of good liquor. Of course, the sheriff hears the commotion and comes a'runnin'. Natural, he knows hit's Rufus's truck, so he arrests Rufus and turns him over to the Fed'ral boys. Rufus tells Bernie he's a'gonna git him when he gits out, so Bernie hain't been seed around these parts since Rufus got out. Paw says that iffen you removed the fools and the moonshiners from Hogwaller, you wouldn't have enough people left to have a good fight. I know Burl and his boys are glad to see Rufus back. They says they hain't had a good drink since Rufus done got sent to prison.

And speaking of the Poindexters, Delilah has been doing some baking out of her house. She makes them little cookies and candies and puts them into a bag and ties a little ribbon around them. She takes them into town and the stores buys them. She's making a tidy little sum of money when she can keep them brothers away from the goods. She said she got the idee to do this when she were away in the big city. I bet she could be one of yore Designin' Wimmen. Do you need anyone else in yore club? She brung me by some of her peanut brickle and hit shore were lairpsome. I think she has designs on me, too, but I'm a'stayin' as fer away as I can. I tolt Maw I didn't have to be hit in the head with a bag of hammers to knows when I'se being played like a fish.

Wal, my eddication is coming along. I've had Maw checking on gitting me a chance to take that GED test. I'm not sure whut hit is, but I has to pass hit before I can git into school. I figger once I git in, I should sail right along with the head I've got on my shoulders. I'se got a natural wit as you can tell, so's I should make friends easy enough wherever I goes and friends will help me iffen I needs hit.

I gots to go. I think I hear some of Delilah's peanut brickle calling me from the kitchen. Since yore a chef, mebbe I could send you some of Delilah's treats and sees whut you thanks about them.

Yores til the cookie crumbles,

Clem

Clem and the GED People

Clem Clodhopper
Rural Route 1
Hogwaller Arkansaw

GED Testing Center
1201 Turner Street
Little Rock, Arkansaw

Dear GED People,

My name is Clem Clodhopper and I want to take yore test whut would allow fer me to go to a school of higher learning. I has graduated from the third grade. and I feels like I could do well on yore test. I could not complete all eight grades of school as I were holping my paw on the farm at the time. I am pert near 30 years old, and I can't stay here in Hogwaller the rest of my natural life. I knows that thar's a lot of thangs that I need to learn iffen I'se to git a good job outside these hills. I have heard of tooters who are people whut can holp me with some of the thangs that I did not git to in school. Do you know whut I'm talking about? Do I hire the tooters or do you jist send them to me? Iffen you would write me back and let me know wheres to go and take the test and how to git them tooters, I would thank you kindly.

Maw and Paw says to wish you a good day. They's been over to Granny Birdwell's house to holp her out since she fell and hurt her tail bone the tother day. Seems she were a herding home her cow to be milked, and Ole Lulu took to balking on her, stopping here and there to eat some tender grass she fount along the fence. Wal, Granny prodded her to move along, but Lulu had a mind of her own and jist kept a'chewing on that grass. Granny got mad, don't you know, and whacked her a good one with a stick and Lulu jumped, which startled Granny awful bad, and she fell and rolled down the hill. Wal, she jist laid there a mite and Lulu jist kept on eating and paying no mind at all to Granny's perdickamint.

71

Have you seed them Lassie movies wheres Timmy gits into all kinds of shapes and Lassie has to git him out? Like he falls down a well and Lassie gits him a rope or runs and tells his paw by barking to come help? I never have figgered out how Timmy's paw can understand dog talk. Anyways, that boy gits in more trubble and pore ole Lassie and his paw have to git him out. And this goes on every day jist at 6:00 P.M. You could set yore watch to the trubbles he gits into. Wal, whut I'm a'gittin at is thar's a big difference betwixt a cow and a dog. Now, ole Lulu warn't about to run anywhere and git help. She were purty happy jist chewing on that grass and she had jist been walloped with a big stick, which might have throwed her holping instink off a tad. So Granny jist lays there amoanin' and a'yellin' fer somebidy in this little high pitched voice. And don't you know that Joe Jenkins is the one to find her. Now Joe ain't got no time to fool with her, so he jist keeps on a'walkin'. Then along comes Pete Owens and he's carting home some groceries fer his own granny and he can't holp her. Wouldn't you know that the next person to find her is Burl Poindexter. Can you see whut I'm a'gittin' at? Now Burl ain't no good Samatarian, but he stops and holps Granny to her feet and gives her a limb to lean on so's she can git home. Granny walks on home though it takes her a tolerable spell to git there. I thank Burl should have holped a little more than he did, but being Burl, he doesn't put hisself out a whole heap. I don't know if that will put a star in Burl's crown, but at least he helped as best he knowed how.

Wal, Granny is laid up and Maw and Paw are there for her needs. As you can see, us Clodhoppers tries to be good neighbors when we can. I hope you'uns are helping type folks also. I would be much obliged iffen you would send me whut I need very soon so's I can take yore test and git out of Hogwaller.

Yores til the spring breaks,

Clem

The GED's Reply

September 12, 2002

GED Testing Center
1201 Turner Street
Little Rock, Arkansas

Mr. Clem Clodhopper
Rural Route 1
Hogwallow, Arkansas

Dear Mr. Clodhopper:

We are most pleased to be able to assist you in the furtherance of your educational pursuits. Obviously, you have had some trials in obtaining these admirable goals. There is a GED testing that will be conducted at Pine Grove High School in Pine Grove, Arkansas, on December 14. That is the closest testing center to Hogwallow. We suggest that in the interim you hire a tutor to assist you in getting up to date on the advances that have taken place in the educational realm since your unfortunate departure from academia back in the third grade. You seemed to be highly motivated, and it is our wish that you fare well on the exam. If there is anything further that we can do to help you, please do not hesitate to let us know. In regard to your other query, yes, we here at the GED Testing Center are pleased to say that we watched the Lassie movies many years ago, and we agree that we do not know how Lassie and Timmy's father communicated so well with each other. We are sure that there have been many experiments done over the years to test theories as to the plausibility of such a thing occurring with such frequency as it seemed to happen in the Lassie series. Furthermore, it is our hope that you tell Granny Birdwell that we wish for her a speedy recovery.

Sincerely Yours,

Geoffrey Spurgeon
Testing Coordinator

Peg Legs and Whale Bone

September 17, 2002

Dear Miss Amelia,

Wal, I has gone and done hit. I signed up to take that GED test, and the GED folks has writ back and says I can take hit in December. After they read my letter, they was pretty strong in their belief that I needs one of them tooters. Since I'm going to have to git up to snuff on grades four through eight in three months, I reckon they's right. I thank I can do hit with the right tooter. Paw is one of the smartest people in the holler, but he ain't real strong in book larning. Maw can read and write a little, but not much better'n me. I have talked to the widow Plumlee who runs the local Hogwaller Liberry. You remember I tolt you about our liberry which has fifteen books, but Mrs. Watson passed away and left her liberry of five books to the Hogwaller Liberry, making hit twenty books now.

Howsomeever, they didn't have one of them books you said I ort to read named **Moby Dick** so they had to borry hit from the Pine Grove High School Liberry. Hit's one of them classics like **War and Peace** and **Gone with the Wind** which you done told me to read. I don't thank I can make hit through them books if they's like **Moby Dick**. I wouldn't have time to git much else done. Wal, I done read through **Moby Dick** with Maw's help, but I hain't shore I understand all I know about hit. It seems that Melville feller went out of his way to say in a hunnerd words what Paw can say in five. And the words he used! I ain't never seed sich a thang. Maw and me came to the opinion that he must have made some of them up. I can tell a fish story in a lot lesser words, and most folks would be able to understand hit. And that story about ole Ahab a'chasin' that whale all over the ocean don't make no sense a'tall. Hit's a big body of water and thar's a lot of them whales he could have chased. It appears he had one of them abcesses with that white whale.

But mainly, I enjoyed that part about Ahab having a peg leg. Now that's real life cause I knows a man here in the holler who has the same thang, exceptin' he didn't lose his real leg to no fish and his'n is made of wood instead of whale bone. Hit were the strangest thang how hit happened. His name is Homer Wiley and he lives a few houses over in the holler. Hit seems Homer were out one Sunday clearing some brush and trees, and he had one of them chipper thangs whut grinds up wood. Wal, Homer was working along and a'dreamin' and a'meditatin' when the machine jammed up. Homer climbs upon that machine and starts poking it with a stick to unclog the thang, but that hain't working a'tall, so's he climbs up on her and jumps up and down on hit and, boy howdy, that thang takes off and makes a grab at Homer, and his leg is sucked down into that machine. You are too delicate to hear the details, but hit were a mess. He were lucky that he only lost his leg. Them doctors send Homer all the way to Little Rock to see iffen they can stick that leg back on, but they's not much there, whut with it being tore up purty good. So Homer winds up with one of them peg legs like ole Ahab. He gits around good and don't seem to have slowed down none, but he don't fool much with machines now. He says them thangs are too quick to make a grab at you, so he's done with machines. Maw says that's whut happens when you work on the Lord's day and that Homer should have been in church. She says the Lord was mad at Homer and was making an example, don't you know. Paw said the Lord twernt mad a'tall, and that He jist didn't give Homer enough common sense. Paw is always looking at the practical side of thangs. Anyhow, you sees whut I'm a'gittin' at. Leave thangs along that can make a grab at you, like that whale Moby Dick fer example. Anyways, it were a purty good book, and if them GED people ask any questions about that book, I can do them up right.

Miss Amelia, there's one other thang bothering me. You said you would like to come to Hogwaller to do some research for yore magazine. Now, Maw's going to want you to stay at her house whilst yore here, and I ain't got no truck with that a'tall exceptin' there could be a problem. Maw fancies herself the best cook in Hogwaller and kind of the head of the social circle since the saloon ladies messed up her hair and she had to wear a scarf and a big hat whut was a big hit with the ladies of the church and they started wearing them too and Maw became sort of the fashion expert in Hogwaller and stands atop the social heap in these parts, don't you see? Here you come to Hogwaller and yore a high muck a muck with cooking and writing and gadgetical thangs and it could cause Maw to backslide a mite in the eyes of them wimmen having such a famous person as yoreself around. Now, Maw won't say so her own self, but I knows Maw and she don't cotton to playing second fiddle. Mebbe you could lay low on the high tone cooking and let Maw handle them chores jist for yore own safety and my peace of mind. She's been a'sweepin' and a'dustin' like mad looking forward to yore arrival. I tolt her hit might be some time afore you could make hit down here, but she hain't taking no chances. Anyways, keep in mind what I said about the cooking if you don't keer. In the meantime, I will be gittin' smarter by using my tooter to help me prepare for the GED test. Wish me luck.

Yores til the tooter toots,

Clem

Amelia's Advice on Studying

Dear Clem,

Of course, I would put first any thoughts you have on my impending visit to Hogwallow. If you feel your mother needs to take the lead in household endeavors such as cooking, I will defer to your wishes. I do not in any way want to demean what your mother does as a cook or in the social activities of Hogwallow. I am there as an observer and writer only. I thought that I might prepare a simple meal to help out while I was there since I do not wish to be a burden. If you feel this will in any way be an affront to your mother's culinary skills, I most certainly will not plan on cooking while I am there.

Now that we have settled that matter, I wish to comment briefly on your preparation for the GED. There is no substitute for diligent study, but you have a very brief time to prepare. I do not like to take shortcuts, but you do not have time to do all the reading you will need to do, so I am enclosing a booklet on how to prepare for the GED. It gives sample questions and answers and gives you information on how to take the test and how to prepare for the different sections. In addition, I am sending some synopses of major literary works for you to peruse. It is a shortcut, of course, and no way a substitute for reading these great classics, but time is of the essence. I fear that your English skills may not be on par with what you will encounter on the test, so I have sent samples of what you might receive on the language skills. Study all the samples I send you diligently, and you should be fine. The tutor is an excellent idea and I hope you follow through on finding someone skillful enough to guide you through the quagmire of examples that I will send to you.

My magazine has agreed to let me do research on the culture of your region. Of course, I will be primarily looking at the social aspect, which will deal with family relationships, family customs, meal preparation, etc. I will look at the environment of the area such as cleanliness, farming methods, water sources, etc. Other areas will include churches, schools, social activities, and so on. It will be a busy time for me and I am planning to spending at least a month there. I would like to stay in different homes while I am there and not impose on your mother the entire time. Staying with different families will give me a broader spectrum of family life, as it may differ from one household to another. If you could talk to your neighbors and let them know about the purpose of my visit and ask them if they would be willing to house me, I would appreciate it so much. I look forward to hearing from you on this matter.

Affectionately yours,

Amelia

Clem Plans for Amelia's Visit

October 2, 2002

Dear Miss Amelia,

Hit has caused quite a ruckus around here whut with you coming to our little holler. I hain't see so much commotion since Penelope Pennymaker eloped with Seth Jenkins. Penelope is only the purtiest girl in Hootin' Holler. She is right up there with Delilah Poindexter on the looksome scale. Wal, Seth is an old Hogwaller boy and about the homeliest poor thang that God ever created. The Pennymaker's was right upset when they discovered that their only daughter had eloped with not only the ugliest boy in the area, but he was also from Hogwaller, which they despises. Hootin' Holler and Hogwaller has always been big rivals in corn shuckings, county fairs, hog calling, or anythang that has to do with bragging rights. Wal, Penelope was the homecoming queen at Hootin' Holler, and pore old Seth's only claim to fame was growing the biggest pum'kin in Hogwaller history. It warn't exactly a match made in heaven. But Penelope saw somethang in Seth that must have went past looks, so's they eloped and nobody knows where they went. Old man Pennymaker has the sheriff and the dogs out looking, but they ain't going to find Seth if he don't want to be fount. That boy knows these parts like a hound knows fleas. I don't thank we've seed the end of this story yit.

Anyways, yore coming to Hogwaller is about as important as any elopement. I've filled yore request of finding families whut would take you in whilst yore here. Natural, Maw and Paw (and me) wants you to stay with them for the first week. Maw has a lot of thangs planned for you to do. She is going to do some canning, and she thanks you could be a big help. She wants to make lye soap which she says she'll give you a batch fer it will make yore skin as young as a baby's bottom. We'll kill some hawgs and Paw will let you do the shooting if you wants to. I tolt him that you wanted to be a part of all the doings around here, so he said that shooting and butchering hogs will be chores you will want to do. I'm a'goin' to take you to a squaredance in

79

Hootin' Holler whilst yore here. I can cut a mean dosie do when them fiddles gits to squealing. I ain't bad to look at and I don't drank or chaw baccer, so you could do worser.

Now the second week you gits to stay with Reverend Johnson and his wife. You remembers Reverend Johnson who I tolt you was going to marry Cecil who we thought was Celeriac but twernt a'tall and Annabelle Tucker who he had been a'sparking on the sly unbeknownst to her paw who caught them and was going to shoot Cecil but instead made them git hitched by Reverend Billings from Hootin' Holler because Brother Johnson had one of them coronas which almost kilt him. Wal, he seems to be fit as a fiddle and they's happy to put you up fer a week. Brother Johnson will tell you about all the church doings, and his wife makes one of the best rhubarb pies you ever sunk yore gums into. Brother Johnson can talk a blue streak and when he gits going, you kin sneak away for an hour and when you gits back, he's still a'talkin' and never knowed you left. So you won't have to worry about being one of them conservationists because he will do all the talking.

The third week you will be staying with the widow Plumlee, who you remembers is the liberrian at the Hogwaller Liberry whut had fifteen books until old Miss Watson died and left it five more whut made it twenty. Now Miss Plumlee is about yore age. Her husband passed away some three years ago from unknown causes that I ain't going to try and explain in this here letter cause they were a bit strange. After her husband died, the Widow Plumlee never got hitched agin. She took to reading all the books in the liberry, and don't you know she has read all fifteen, plus the books Mrs. Watson left. Kin you imagine reading twenty books? If they's all like **Moby Dick,** she can't have much space left in her brain. Anyways, she is a nice gal and you two will git along good.

Now, the fourth week will be the one whut has me in some doubts. I don't thank you kin leave the holler without meeting the Poindexters. I would not want you to go within miles of the place if Delilah warn't there. But you wants a full experience, I thank, is whut you said, so I'se giving hit to you. Paw has talked to Burl who has agreed to let you come there fer a week. I thank he feels he owes hit to Paw.

Delilah, is jist beside herself. Now they's going to be another woman around fer a bit, and she won't have to be the only female in a house full of men. She's fixin' up the little shack in the back of the

80

house fer you. They stores meat in there during the winter, but it will be all tidy when you git there. Delilah will see to hit. All the Poindexter boys are slobbering at the mouth. They hain't seed any wimmen 'cepting Delilah and some of the local gals, who knows them too good to give them the time of day. They's harmless but awful bothersome, especially with there being so many of them and so few of you. Delilah will want you to see her baking doings that she has started. Them little cookies and candies she makes has been selling like fly swallers in an outhouse if you gits my drift. She thanks that with yore gadgetical mind that you can come up with some way to git them out faster. She is willing to go to New York and let yore Designin' Wimmen be partners jist so's she can git her candy and cookies to the big city. She says that in a big city like New York, she could sell upwards to three or four dozen a day. I thank that Delilah jist wants to git out of Hogwaller. Iffen she makes money to boot, well, that jist makes the cheese more binding, don't you know.

Let me know yore plans and I'll git the tree a'shakin' here.

Yores til the cheese molds,

Clem

Politics and Dog Fights

October 15, 2002

Dear Miss Amelia,

I hain't heered from you fer a while. I hope everythang is going good in yore neck of the woods. I'se gotten kind of used to hearing from you so don't forgit to write since I consider us to be pen pals now. I knows thangs in a big city like New York can be worrisome, but let me know how thangs are going whilst yore gitting ready for yore trip here.

Wal, hit's almost here. Folks is lining up and taking sides. Dirty lundry is being throwed every whichaway. If a person has a skelton in his closet, hit's a'rattlin' to beat the band. Yep, election day is almost here, and thangs have heated up considerable. Why, even the dogs have gone electional. The tother day Cecil's dog was jist walking through town down to Jake's butcher shop to git a bone as he always does on Wensday, and jist as he turned the corner by the feed and grain, there sat Melville T's big old bulldog. Now, nobody in the holler has a bulldog 'cepting Melville T. They's knowed to be mean, and only Melville T. would keep a mean dog. Cecil's dog is jist an old coonhound, but he has spirit and he don't back down from nuthing.

Wal, Melville T's dog starts to a'growlin' and a'diggin' dirt and throwing it every which a ways like some bull whut's going to charge. Boomer, that's Cecil's dog, don't you know, looks at him like he's bored and not worth his time, cause he's got a big bone a'waiting. Jist as he gits his back turned, Melville T's dog grabs him from behind. Then, Boomer gloms on to Beauregard, that's Melville T's dog, and git's a holt of his leg. And there they are, jist a'whirlin' and a'rollin' and dust jist a'flyin'. By this time a crowd has gathered to watch whut happens. Nothing git's a crowd together faster'n a good dog fight. Soon, Cecil and Melville T. git there cause they've heered whut was going on, and then the real ruckus begins. Cecil says Melville T. has a killer dog, and hit's jist a matter of time until he hurts someone. Melville T. says that Cecil's dog started the whole thang and before

82

you can say catawampus, they starts in to pounding on each other, and that gits everybody taking sides and you've got dogs a'bitin' and a'growlin' and men a'cussin' and a'fightin' and the women folk are a'cryin' and a'tryin' to git everybody apart. And then hit happened.

Jim Conklin's boy Charlie tries to break up the dogs and he gits bit all over. He's gitting rolled around and Beauregard has glommed on to his arm. By this time the sheriff has arrived, and he has to shoot Beauregard to git him off Charlie. They has to pry his mouth off Charlie's arm don't you know. Wal, Melville T. threatens to sue Cecil and the sheriff and half of Hogwaller for killing his dog. Jim Conklin threatens to sue Melville T. for having a killer dog. Cecil is a'spittin' blood and a'callin' Melville T. a lunitick and a instigator. And Paw's write-in campaign is gitting better all the time. But hit was bound to happen, the fightin' and name-calling and all. Hit had been a'brewin' for weeks. Cecil had got one of them ads on our local radio whut is HAWG radio broadcasting. He had heard that hit was the thang in big cities to advertise on radio and television and everybody in Hogwaller has a radio. They like to tune in on Satidday nights to listen to Melvin Potts and the Pot Bangers, which is our local band. They has one record out called "She's My Gal Cause Nobody Else Will Have Her", and hit has sold several copies. So Cecil pays to have a slogan broadcast on the air. Hit says "Vote Cecil Sims for Mayor, the right man for Hogwaller." He even come up with a ditty to sang whut folks could remember. Hit goes, "Vote for Cecil and help Hogwaller. You'll git more fer every dollar. Come out early, don't be hicks, and vote for Cecil on November 6."

Now, Melville T. ain't one to be outdid, so's he not only buys air time, but he challenges Cecil to a debate. Wal, Cecil agrees and they git's a panel of people to ask questions so's they can debate them. Old Miss Larabee, who runs the local dry goods store, wanted to know whut they was a'goin' to do about taxes. Cecil says that taxes is whut makes America great and he is all fer them, which draws a few catcalls from the crowd. Melville T. says he is aginst all taxes, and nobody will have to pay them if he is elected. He don't go into a lot of detail about how he plans to do hit, which is jist like a politician, Paw says. They says whut you want to hear and when they gits elected, they say they never said any sich a thang. Mr. Barlow, the local barber, says that bissness has fallen off considerable since the recession has hit the holler. He thanks the new mayor should bail out his bissness since people don't have to have haircuts and would druther buy food and cut their own hair. Cecil says to cut back on days in the shop and mebbe expand to selling soaps and creams and sich thangs. Melville T. says that he will ask Warshington to send him a couple of million dollars to give to bissnesses that hain't doing good. He says that's the true American way. Try something and git yore money from hit, and iffen it fails, have the guv'ment to take keer of hit. Hit didn't take me long to see that common sense warn't a big part of Melville T.'s campaign.

Then Paw stands up and asks whut they was a'goin' to do about the Poindexter house which sets over Shankey Branch. Cecil says they can do whut is called eminent domain. Now, we knows Cecil is smart about sich thangs, being eddicated and all, and he says that means the city of Hogwaller would have the right to take the property that Burl owns and give him fair money fer hit since hit is polluting the dranking water. Wal, this wakes Burl up real quick. He purty much sleeps through any meeting, but he got alert real quick and tolt Cecil he warn't going to take his property as long as he had guns and enough powder to put a stop to trespassers. Melville T. tried to calm Burl down by saying nobody was planning to take his home. Melville T. knew he would lose several votes iffen he didn't tell Burl whut he wanted to hear.

Wal, the upshot of the debate was that Cecil was Cecil and Melville T. was Melville T. and hit was purty much a waste of time. I agree with Paw. Jist take all the politicians and put them in a sack and hang the sack in a high tree out in the woods. The first one to figger out how to git out of the sack and down to the ground without breaking his neck wins the election. Hit makes as much sense to me as debating and would be a whole lot more interesting. I'm jist glad the election is only a short time away. Mebbe thangs will git back to normal after hit's over. Wal, I'm going to git back to studying for that GED test. Widow Plumlee, the liberrian, is tootering me. She sits real close while she's a'goin' over them verbs and nouns and sich. I tolt her I could hear real good and she didn't have to sit that close, but hit seemed to be easier for her, so's I let hit go. I can tell I'm gitting smarter, because my head hurts after I gits through being tootered. Pushing all that book learning in there at one time has to take up a lot of space and would hurt anybody's head. I'm hitting the hay early tonight. Five o'clock comes awful early, and I have to meet the folks that Paw hired to drill fer water after I eat one of Maw's big breakfasts. I'll write agin soon.

Yores til the water spouts,

Clem

Parental Guidance

October 25, 2002

Dear Clem,

Yes, it has been a while since I have written. I have been extremely busy preparing for my trip to your fair hamlet. This is quite an undertaking for me since I will be away for a month. I must pack so many things to wear to all the different functions that will be taking place while I am there. I cannot let your mother down by not looking my best at all times. Then of course I must educate someone to do my job while I am gone. The temporary hire must be able to do my duties here which is an enormous responsibility since I practically run the place by myself.

I have informed my mother and father of my intentions of making the trip to Hogwaller. I cannot say without blushing the comments my mother made. I will try to do so at another time. Needless to say, she is against the trip and would forbid me to go if she had the power to do so. My father is very laid back concerning the matter. He just tells me to pack some warm clothes as it will get chilly in the hills this time of year. He also says to be careful to avoid the wildlife in the area, especially bears. Do you have bears in Hogwallow? Do I need to bring a whistle and bear repellant?

Keep me apprised about the election since it is the biggest news going on in your town. I want to know about the area before I get there so I can converse with the locals. Knowing about the politics of the area as well as the people will make me more acceptable in their eyes. Oh,I do hope they like me.

I must go for I have so much more to do in the next few weeks. I will continue to write though not as much as I would wish. Please keep sending me letters because they really brighten my day.

Affectionately,

Amelia

Election Day

November 7, 2002

Dear Miss Amelia,

Wal, hit's over! The mayor's election is over. I'se going to keep you in suspense fer a few minutes whilst I tells you about some of the going's on during the election. First, let me tell you about whut Melville T. was up to. He had put up posters all around the Hogwaller Elementary School where all the voting was a'bein' done. He had stuck some of them right on the posts of the building, and the sheriff had tolt him that hit were illegal to do that. He had to move them signs or he would hold Melville T. in contempt. Melville T. was hotter'n a firecracker, but he moved the signs. Then he stood around the voting area and was a'talkin' to people as they came in to vote, and the sheriff tolt him he would have to move hisself from the voting area. Wal, this got Melville T. even hotter. He got to talking about how it were un-American to take away a feller's rights like that. He had free speech and he would git the sheriff's job when he won the election. He were jist a'goin' on and the sheriff said he can't do that around where people are voting, and Melville T. said he had his rights and the sheriff arrested him fer contempt and was a'goin' to take him to jail. Melville T. said he had a right to vote first, and the sheriff let him go into one of the booths to vote.

Wal, whilst the sheriff warn't looking, Melville T. slipped out the back door and cut a beeline fer the Poindexter place. When he git's there, he tells Burl and his boys to git some of their moonshine and head to the school. When they gits to the school, they is to hand out free samples to some of the big drinkers in the holler, which includes most of the men. Hit don't take no genus to know he were a'buyin' votes. But that's not the worstest of hit. Hit was fount out later by Sheriff Tate that Melville T. has Burl to send Harold and Darryl to Cecil's house where they is to loosen a bolt on one of the wheels of his wagon so's hit will come off while he is a'drivin' hit to vote. Thataway Cecil and Annabelle won't git to vote, don't you know.

Hit's jist like one of them cowboy programs on television where's a bad guy looses a bolt of a wheel on a wagon, and the horses are a'runnin' away and the woman is a'yellin' and a'cryin' to save her and here comes Gene Autry out of nowheres and jist as the wagon goes over the hill and tumbles and crashes with parts a'flyin' everwhere, Gene snatches the woman from the wagon and saves her and all the time he's jist a'singin' right along. I never have figgered out why them cowboys had to spend so much time a'savin' wimmen when there was so many bad guys a'loosenin' wheels that they needed to stop. Them females in the old West was the most helpless thangs I've ever seed. Nary a one could stop a team of mules or ride a horse without hit running away and iffen they was a'bein' chased, they'd lose a shoe or fall down and act all helpless. No self-respecting hill woman would ever act thataway.

Wal, I don't thank that Harold and Darryl wanted to hurt Cecil and Annabelle, so's they did jist enough to break the wagon down. Now, Cecil and Annabelle they was a'drivin' along and the wheel comes off and they is stranded out there. Don't you know Annabelle would'a fit right in with them wild West wimmen. That gal ain't got no grit a'tall. She's a'goin' on about how's they is going to die there without water ner food, and hit's only three miles from the school and one mile back to their house. Cecil is a'cussin' because hit will be too late fer them to vote. Meanwhile, Burl and his boys are a'servin' whiskey to voters and Melville T. has slipped back into town. Hours later when Sheriff Tate gits back to town, he will find Melville T. in a jail cell. He has turned hisself in on his own.

Now, all that is strange enough, but git this. Cecil has walked and half carried Annabelle to the school, but when they gits there, them polls has closed. Cecil is madder'n a stirred up hornet's nest with nobody to sting. He wants to talk to the sheriff, but the sheriff is a'lookin' fer Melville T. and the only other person he could complain to is the mayor and that's Melville T. at the present time, and he ain't present at the time. None of the workers at the polls has the power to let Cecil and Annabelle vote, so Cecil heads out to find the sheriff who is a'lookin' fer Melville T.

The upshot of hit all is when the sheriff gits to town, Cecil is right behind him and they both arrive at the jail to find Melville T. has locked hisself in, so's the sheriff's job is already done.

By this time folks has gotten back to town, when all of a sudden

Tom Simpkins comes a'runnin' to tell the sheriff that the ballot box has been stole. Hit seems that the box were being brought in to have the votes counted and Caleb Tarwater, the official vote counter, was knocked in the head and the box were stole. Natural, everybody thought of Burl and his boys, but all of them were seed at the school giving out whiskey. Paw thanks hit's Melville T.'s doing, but nobody can prove hit and he were locked up in jail. My vote goes to Burl. I thank he seed how the voting were a'goin' and he knowed that Melville T. had to be elected if he wanted to keep his house where hit is. Burl is as sneaky as a fox in a hen house, and I think he took the box and dumped hit at the edge of town. They fount the box a few hours later with the lid all smashed in and votes scattered every whichaway. All the folks that voted was counted when they voted. They was ninety-nine adults who voted. That only left Cecil and Annabelle and Granny Birdwell who didn't git to vote. You remembers Granny Birdwell whut was a'brangin' her cow home to milk and hit were being stubborn and eating grass and she hit the cow with a stick which jumped and bumped Granny and she rolled down the hill and hurt her tail bone and the cow were too dumb to git help and Burl was a good Samatarian and holped her. I'm a tad ashamed to say this, but I was tolt by Paw to pick her up to vote and I forgot hit in all the excitement. So she didn't git to vote. All the slips were accounted fer so whoever tried to destroy the votes did a pore job. Caleb said the votes was official and the election were over.

I guess I'se kept you a'waiting' long enough. Melville T. got twenty votes. I figgers that he voted fer hisself and Emma Jean Watson would vote fer her paw. Burl and his boys would vote fer Melville T. and mebbe Delilah. I figgers he got a few votes from the shine he handed out. Cecil got thirty-two votes. Most people figgered Cecil had the brains to be mayor but he had a hard time gitting along with folks, being uppity about his eddication and all, and Annabelle warn't going to be a good first lady fer shore. Now git this! Paw had forty-seven write in votes. Paw tolt me he didn't vote for hisself. He figgered a feller was tooting his own horn too much voting fer hisself, so he voted fer Cecil.

Of course, Cecil and Melville T. has demanded a recount. Cecil says him and Annabelle didn't git to vote because they was waylaid and the votes had been tampered with. Melville T. blamed everybody including the sheriff fer all manner of wrongdoings and said he wanted a investigation into being harristed by the sheriff. I thank that means he were irritated by the sheriff's doings. Paw don't know whut to make of hit all, and he's jist trying to figger out whut hit is exactly a mayor does. Melville T. didn't do nothing but sit around his house and sip whiskey and smoke cigars. Paw thanks hit's more than that so's he's going to talk to the Widow Plumlee about whut a mayor does. She's got a book on guv'ment in her liberry so she can read about hit. I don't thank hit's much more than good common sense and treating people kindly when they comes to you fer help. Paw says his first act of bissness will be to git Burl's house moved off Shankey Branch Crik. I guess what goes round comes round and Burl is a'payin' fer his sins. Paw says he thanks he will whitewash his house because he wants to live in the white house. Haw! Haw! Paw kills me sometimes. I must git my sense of humor from him. Anyways, all the excitement is over and thangs can git back to normal agin. When you makes yore trip, you will be staying with the new mayor fer a week. Don't let it go to yore head.

Yore election reporter from Hogwaller,

Clem

Getting Back to Nature and Diabetes

November 14, 2002

Dear Miss Amelia,

After all the thangs that were a'goin' on in Hogwaller the last few days, I had to git into the hills and hug a tree like them folks out in Californee. Paw is all caught up in his new job, Maw has some ailments that I will tell you about, Cecil and Melville T. hain't cooled off much yit since losing to Paw in the election. So I took Ole Buford and went into the hills. You remembers I tolt you about Buford branging back the duck whut Paw shot on the river and we writ you and asked for yore recipe fer duck on a orange. Wal, Buford is a good dog and a good traveling buddy. He won't talk me to death and he don't eat much, and all he asks is a little attention now and agin and he's as happy as a rabbit in a turnip patch. So's I takes my rifle, calls ole Buford, and we heads off into the hills. You knows I can git high up in these hills and smell that clean mountain air and there ain't nothing like hit. The trees are coloring up something fierce with bushes and flowers with dabs of reds, and purples, and yellows. Orangy colors are jist flowing like a river, the mountain laurel is everwhere, the streams are full and rushing along from the latest rains, and I'se as close to heaven as I can git on earth.

Do you like the mountains, Miss Amelia? Have you laid out under the heavens at night with them stars jist a'shinin' and that ole moon looking like you could reach right up and touch hit with yore fingers? Have you watched the clouds float acrost the sky and listened to the wind blowing through the pines with a shushing sound so soft that hit puts you to sleep? I listen to the howl of the coyotes, and the "who, who" of the ole hooty owl, and that bobcat crying in the distance, and yore symphanies in New York don't play music that purty. There ain't no cars, no trains, no city noises, no sickly smells here. They's no politics, no wars, no crime, no hungry children, no worries about how folks is going to survive from one day to the next.

Hit's times like this when I thanks I might not go back home a'tall, but jist live here. Mebbe build a small cabin close to a stream and me'n ole Buford will jist live offen the land like folks used to do afore the guv'ment started paying folks not to farm and started giving us thangs like welfare so folks would git lazy and shiftless. I could raise a little garden with cabbages and maters and mebbe some of them sweet taters that I likes so much when Maw fries them up in the morning. I could plant some fruit trees and bushes and have fruit in the summer. I loves them big ripe blueberries and blackberries that are so juicy that the tongue turns as blue as the berries theirselves. I could jist lay around or take walks through the fields and watch a momma doe teach her young'un how to survive or watch a momma bird teach her small ones how to jump from a nest and never seem to worry they won't make hit. Somehows, they do, and I thank I could too. But then I git to thanking about Maw and Paw and how they might need me and I knows my place is in Hogwaller. At least fer now.

Speaking of Maw, she hain't doing so well. She's been awful tarred lately, and Doc Whittaker warn't having any luck a'tall figgering out whut was wrong. Maw don't have a lazy bone in her body, but her pep were all gone. So's Doc Whittaker sends Maw to Little Rock to have some tests done. And come to find out she's diabetical. Now, I only knows one other person in the holler who is diabetical and that is Jebediah Huckleby. Jebediah likes to drank moonshine a lot and he gits him a gallon ever time Rufus Sweeney makes a run. You remembers Rufus who was making a run of shine and Bernie Crawford who likes to drank too much was a'hidin' in back of the truck and when Rufus parks the truck on the street in Hogwaller, hit comes out of gear and rolls back into the feed and grain loading dock and Bernie bails out and all them bottles rolls out of the truck and breaks all over the street and the sheriff arrests Rufus fer running shine. Wal, you know how much sugar is used in making shine I'm shore. Hit's a passel. And Jebediah he likes them mashed taters and hog jowl and cakes and cookies and moon pies and red drinks, and he'll drank two dozen of them RC colas in a day. So he got porely and they had to take him to the hospital where's they tolt him he were diabetical. They tolt him he would have to quit the shine and the cathead biscuits and the cakes and cookies and the moon pies and taters and RC's and sich because they had too much sugar and carbyhydrants. Wal, Ol' Jeb figgers a life without them pleasures ain't

92

worth living, so's he goes right on with whut he was a'doin'. The first thang he knows he's lost some toes and then he loses a laig, and that diabetical sitiation was jist a'climbin' up his body. I don't know whut he would uv lost next afore he decided to do whut the doctors was a'tellin' him.

Anyhow, Maw knows a heap better than Jebediah, and she don't eat like that nohow. She's a small woman by Hogwaller standards. Doc Whittaker says hit may be one of them heretic thangs wheres you git hit from your ancestors. Anyways, Maw has to watch whut she eats, so she has to cut back on all the baking she likes to do, but she still fixes aplenty fer me and Paw and we's supporting her while she's diabetical by being extra nice and helping out with her work until she gits her pep back.

Hit seems that sickness in one form or tother is always with us. When hit makes good people sick, hit jist seems more awful. Paw says hit rains on the just and the unjust, which I reckon is right. Iffen I had the right to ask God for anythang, hit would be to give them diseases to the bad people who never do any good for nobody but theirselves. Maw goes to the church every time the doors opens, she holps people when they gits sick, she hain't never turnt nobody away from her door when they needed help. She teaches Sunday school to the little'uns, and she hain't never seed a bad child she says. So whut does she git for all that good work? She gits diabetical.

Miss Amelia, I knows God has a plan for us, but I shore can't figger hit out. You probly goes to one of them big churches whut knows all the answers. If yore preacher knows whut's going on with that plan, send me the reason bad thangs happen to good people. I'd like to know and I thank hit would give Maw sum comfort, too. Wal, I'm shore my problems is small ones and they will pass. Paw also says the man who hain't got no shoes thanks he's bad off until he meets a man who hain't got no legs. Kind of like Ole Jebediah, I reckon. I'll git out of here. Hit's almost eight o'clock and time for bed. I kin already hear that ol' hooty owl, and I'm longing fer those hills agin. Sleep tight, Miss Amelia.

Longing fer them hills,

Clem

93

Amelia Becomes Flustered

November 22, 2002

Dear Clem,

I was so disconcerted to hear of your dear mother's illness. Fortunately, with the advances made in diabetes research in recent years, your mother can lead a full and productive life with very little inconvenience from the disease if she will follow her doctor's orders. The disease is quite often hereditary and most likely would have happened to your mother regardless of how vigilant she would have been in diet and exercise. Quite often people ignore the warning signs and do nothing to alter their life styles and pay the ultimate price as with your friend Jebediah. Please give her my best.

I am getting prepared for Thanksgiving here. I will be going home to my family in North Carolina. I am not sure that I am looking forward to it. Mother will be trying to talk me out of taking my trip to Hogwallow. Father will be going on and on about the state of the nation, the economy, the President, ad infinitum, and all I will want to do is eat and go to bed. I need rest more than anything. My job is eighteen hours a day and my trip home is my chance to rest up. I know your mother will cook a big feast and there will be peace in your house. I envy you.

Oh, your eloquent words on your escape into nature touched me most deeply! You may be rudimentary in your communication skills, but you have the heart and soul of a poet. I, too, love to get into nature and commune with its various aspects. Henry David Thoreau, the noted transcendentalist and naturalist who wrote the inspired work **Walden**, said, "I went to the woods because I wished to live deliberately, to front only the essential facts of life, and see if I could not learn what it had to teach, and not, when I came to die, discover that I had not lived." Thoreau said it so eloquently, and it is exactly what I wish to do on those days when the pressures of my work and my hectic schedule make me eager to toss it all in and go to some sylvan paradise such as your mountains. I do have my own retreat in the hills of North Carolina close to the Tennessee border. It is a small cabin which belongs to an aunt of mine and a place I hope to inherit in the future. I am the only one in the family who goes there on a regular basis, and I do not believe any other family members have an interest in it. It sits beside a flowing stream in a small glade and has only the basic accoutrements, but they are sufficient for my needs. At night, during the summer I can lie in bed with the windows open and the doors unlocked and need not worry that there is any danger other than some furry denizen of the woods might enter, foraging for food. The smells of the fields and the woods and the sounds of creatures of the night are a balm to my frazzled nerves, an opiate that sends me into the most peaceful slumbers. I, too, have lain under the stars and marveled at the wonders of the universe. I wish I could be there beside you to gaze at the stars in your world. Studying the heavens is much more rewarding if it is done with a friend. Of course, I am talking in the platonic sense only. After all, I was reared with the highest sense of decorum and virtue and would not want my friends to think that such a tryst would be anything other than a scientific observation of the heavens with a friend. Yet, lying there with you in such a setting would enhance certain emotions, I must admit. I can see you there in the moonlight like an Adonis, a veritable sculpture of true manhood. I would be your Aphrodite and love you for your beauty and poetic soul. We would look at the stars, and as the wonder of those magnificent lamps of the heavens filled our souls, slowly our hands would touch and we would be drawn together like…Oh, My! There I go again letting my imagination get the best of me. Pardon me while I moisten my face with a cold towel…

There now, I'm back. I believe I was telling you of my cabin when I digressed earlier. I love the blueberries and other fruit that are so abundant, much as you described in your letter. It is calming to take a large bucket and pick blueberries for hours and never notice the passage of time nor think about those problems in the outside world.

Occasionally, Ben, my neighbor, will happen by and we will talk about the weather or crops or hunting and fishing, those subjects that occupy so much of a person's life in that secluded area. Ben has been known to partake of hallucinogenic substances, and sometimes he does not make the best of sense, but he has a good heart and would do anything for me. And this is true for most of the residents there. I never feel afraid, nor do I worry about thieves, perverts, or sordid characters in those hills. The people who reside there have their own way of living and it is nothing like mine, but that does not make it wrong, just different. I enjoy the contrast for a short time. Their spontaneous nature and gentle and giving spirits make me think of the natives of Hogwallow, and those qualities make me look with even more eagerness to my impending visit there.

I am glad the election went well for your father. I believe he will make a most diligent mayor. I'm sure Burl Poindexter will get his just desserts in whatever form it might come. Those who pervert good for their own gain usually end up with nothing to show for their futile efforts. I do hope that I don't sound too much like a moralist when I go into my tirades, but I do so like to see the virtuous win out and the Poindexters of the world will most certainly reap a bitter harvest when all is said and done. Well, that is my sermon for today, so I will again say adieu and wish you well until I see you in the near future.

Affectionately,

Your stargazing friend, Amelia

Clem Expounds on Religion

December 1, 2002

Dear Miss Amelia,

Hit's getting chilly this time of year here in Hogwaller, but they's still a lot of thangs going on. I went down to the local feed and grain store yestiddy and jist stayed for a mite to ketch up on the local news. You knows how the boys will jist meet and talk and swap knifes and guns and what not. More bissness is conducted at the local feed and grain than anywheres in the world, plus you git to hear all the local gossip. Hit seems that Lester Bumpkus is gitting one of them new John Deere tracters. That's big news here in the holler. Hit's setting there at the feed and grain waiting fer Lester to pick hit up. Hit's the biggest, greenest thang you ever seed. Not many of us hill folk can afford one of them nice machines. Most of the folks here still uses a mule and a plow to turn ground, so this had tongues a'waggin'. Lester hain't no more richer than nobody else in Hogwaller and rumor has hit that he's been growing somethang other than taters. Of course, nobody is going to fault Lester fer trying to make a living, but some folks is concerned that whutever he is a'growin' might find hit's way to some of our local folks, especially the young'uns who don't know no better. Lester were a wild one when he were young, and not too many folks want to mess with him. He's been known to shoot first and ask questions later. So's we jist waits and watches to see whut happens. Sheriff Tate is purty good at his job, and if Lester makes a slip, he will be on him like a duck on a June bug.

The big news is Burl Poindexter is a'goin' to have to move his house. Paw sent one of them official letters to the EPA folks and they has hit Burl with a citation. He has three months to move his house or they will come and tear hit down, so Burl's been moving like a one legged man at a square dance. Of course, with all them boys he's got, they's going to be able to git hit moved quick. So I guess Paw git's the last laugh, as the saying goes. They's no love lost betwixt Burl and Paw, but I don't thank Paw was wanting to git even. He jist wants clean water fer folks in the holler. He's still got the folks drilling fer water on his scrub property jist in case.

The big news in the Poindexter family is Clovis. Hit's jist a'bothering him terrible all the bad thangs his fambly's been a'doin'. You remember when Annabelle was a'givin' a speech fer Cecil fer mayor and somebody chucked a mater and hit her and nobody knew who hit were and later Clovis stood up in church and said, "Hit was me. I did it, Preacher" and Annabelle starting crying and Cecil had to defend Annabelle's honor and started a'punchin' Clovis. Wal, Clovis has fount the Lord. He's taken to reading the Bible twict a day and going to church every Sunday and he's asked Brother Johnson to holp him understand whut the words mean. Jist this past week he was baptized at the First Footwashing Baptist Church of the Second Coming of Hogwaller. Hit were kind of funny to see. Thar stood big ole Clovis, all six foot five inches and three hunnerd pounds, and there stood Brother Johnson who weighs a hunnerd and fifty pounds soaking wet gitting ready to dunk Clovis under the water. He starts to dip Clovis and purty much jist drops him into the water. Clovis comes up coughing and spitting and slanging water everywheres. I thank several folks on the front row got baptized at the same time as Clovis. But he were a good sport about hit. Paw said hit's probably the first time in months he's had that much water on him. I started to laugh but Maw punched me in the ribs and gave Paw one of them looks and Paw jist started humming under his breath. But git this. Now Clovis wants to become a preacher and has asked Brother Johnson to holp him understand the Bible good enough to preach. So three days a week Brother Johnson has Clovis to come in and study the Bible verses with him. I thank Brother Johnson has made a mistake starting Clovis out in the begattings in Genesis. That's pert nigh enuff to keep me from reading the Bible. I thank I would start with somethang interesting like David and that giant feller Goliath. Now that's a good story and hit has a moral. You don't have to be a big feller to win if God is on yore side and you got a good supply of rocks. Now, take Clovis. He's a biggun fer shore, but he hain't going to win people over to the Lord with his size.

And I thank the story of Jonah and the whale is a good story. You has to obey the Lord or He's going to cause you all kind of trouble. I don't thank the Lord in them olden days had a lot of patience. He had a lot to git done, and iffen you didn't listen, He'd chuck you into a whale

98

or into the lion's den or send them locusts and floods and sich. I'm kind of glad He's calmed down a mite, though I believe they's jist as many bad people today that needs them plagues as they was back then. Anyways, I wish Clovis good luck. We don't need folks like the Poindexters causing trouble, and we can't have too many preachers. Unless they's them television preachers whut's into healing and always wanting money fer doing hit. There was this one preacher who said he could heal through the television, and I has to admit I had my doubts untill I found out I was wrong.

Two summers ago, I had got down in my back and I was jist a'crawlin' on the floor to do thangs. Wal, I was jist a'lyin' in the floor one day a'watchin' television, which were about all I could do, when this feller named Ernest Ainsley came on and said he could heal folks whut was a'hurtin'. He was jist a'carryin' on and healing folks right and left. Someone would be holped up to the front and say, "Preacher, I gots this hurting in my hip and I can't walk" and Brother Ainsley would whock that person up side the head and say for them demons to come out. That ole boy would fall backards like he'd been shot and then git up and walk. Then he says for them folks at home who can't be there to lay their hands on the television set and he would heal them. I figgered I didn't have nothing to lose, so I crawls over to the TV and puts my hand on hit. Brother Ainsley tells them demons to come out agin but I don't notice no change, so's I jist crawls back to my pallet and lays down. Now git this. It warn't more'n five minutes until my back was looser'n a noodle. I gits up and walks around better'n ever. When I tells Paw about hit, he jist laughs and tells me I was the first Clodhopper to ever be cured by a television.

Anyways, I thank if Clovis makes hit as a preacher, with those brothers of his'n, he's got a whole flock of heathens there at home he can practice on.

Jist one other bit of news and I'll let you go back to yore woman stuff. Hit's one week and a few days until I takes that GED test and I'se been studying somethang fierce. I been meeting the Widow Plumlee reg'lar three nights a week at the liberry and she's a good tooter. We'se going to meet every night this week to do whut she calls cramming. Widow Plumlee seems to enjoy this tootering work, but she gits real nervous acting when she gits close to me to explain somethang. I tells her I can hear fine and she don't have to sit so close, but she jist prefers hit that way I reckon. Howsomeever, hit's really

99

hard to concentrate when she takes my hand to show me how to read lines and she gits this little hitch in her breathing. I'm not shore whut that's about. It could be one of them allegories that people gits when the trees git all yaller. Folks start to sneezing and wheezing and breathing all funny jist like she's a'doin'. But I thank hit's coming along good and I plans to be ready when them GED fellers git here with that test. I can tell I'se a'gittin' smarter. Hit don't take me near as long to write these letters and you can tell my putting words together is better'n ever. If the Widow Plumlce don't let them allegories git her down, I'll be set.

Wal, I'se going to git back to the books. By the next time you hear from me, I'm a'hopin' to be a real high school graduate.

Yores til the scholar ships,

Clem

Clem and the GED Test

December 15, 2002

Dear Miss Amelia,

Yestiddy, I took that GED test and I'se a mite worried about how I mighta done on hit. Hit were three hours long and I needed every bit of hit to finish. There was a lot of questions that I waren't shore about, but I thank I did alright. Fer example, I writ down one of them language questions to show Widow Plumlee. Hit read "The internet is a world wide network of computers_____easy sharing and transfer of all sorts of information." Then hit gave five choices like this A. that allow for   B. that allows for   C. that allow   D. allow for the   E. allow.   Wal, hit seems unfair that they don't give the right answer which is "whut allows fer." So's I had to pick one of them five answers. I thank the language part might have been the worstest fer me. I throwed in some jokes because I wanted them test people to see I has a sense of humor which is important if you wants folks to like you. Fer an example: How many New York folk does hit take to dress a possum? Hit takes five. Four to hold the critter whilst the other one puts hit on. Haw! Haw! They's bound to like that. I made hit New York people since I knows you have a good sense of humor.

Then I draws some cows and trees and flowers and what not on the test sheet to show off my artery talents. They's going to be impressed, I know fer shore.

The last part of the test were whut they called a essay question. They wanted me to write about some person I knows whut is an inspiration to me. Wal, at first I thought about Paw because he is the best man I knows and he has a good sense of humor and likes to holp folks. But then I thanks of Maw and I figgered she were the best choice. Ever since I was a little baby, my maw has been there for me. When I was jist a young'un, I knows I gave her some fits because I was always running off and gitting into thangs. You know like little boys will do. Nothing bad, but she wouldn't know whars I was and she would worry until she fount me. She would worry that some wild animal would git me or I would fall and brake something. I guess all maws worrys thataway, but mine has a reason. I'se an only child now, but I had a brother once and he were jist like me, always running around and doing boy thangs. Wal, he stepped on a nail whilst prowling around in some old lumber from a house what had been tore down. Now this was some years ago and Doc Whittaker warn't around. My brother got the lockjaw from the nail and he died. This made Maw twice as pertective of me because she thanks she should have been able to prevent Carl from dying. I knows, and I thank she knows, that boys will be boys and you can't watch them ever minute, but you knows how maws are. Hit's a woman's makeup to bear too much of the burden when bad thangs happen in a fambly. She makes shore I goes to church each Sunday even though I'se growed now. She volunteers for ever church activity and calls on the sick when they needs help. She takes care of Paw and the house and even will come over and take care of mine if I needs it. She's a good Christian woman, and so I writ about her on my essay. I hopes them GED people liked hit.

You remembers our postman Jake who got his feet frostbit when he drank too much whilst he was a'deliverin' mail and passed out and lost all his toes on his left foot, cepting his big toe which were a hammertoe with this toenail he couldn't cut and you Designin' Wimmen sent him a gadgetical device what cut hit off? Wal, Jake's in a passel of trouble, don't you know. Hit seems that Jake were delivering more than the mail. You remembers Rufus Sweeney who were a'runnin' shine and he parked his truck in town and hit came out of gear and rolled into the loading dock of the feed and grain and spilt the whiskey he was a'deliverin' and he were arrested by Sheriff Tate? Hit seems that Rufus has more than one way to deliver his goods. Him and Jake were in cahoots and Jake were delivering whiskey fer Rufus on his mail route. Rufus was paying him to deliver his whiskey with the mail. Hit seems the post office people fount out about whut Jake were a'doin' when Missus Henry, who is a teetotaler, got a pint in her mail which were meant fer someone else and turnt hit in to the post office. So Jake's in a heap of trouble and Paw is trying to holp him keep his job. Jake won't tell on Rufus, so's Rufus gits off and no one knows hit's more his doing than Jake's. We all likes Jake and hates to see him in jail or out of a job, being that he is without all his toes. I thank hit should be a hardship case. If I was going to arrest anybody,

102

hit would be Rufus. I don't thank the man has done a honest day's work in his life. Hit's another case of good thangs happen to bad people, but hit will catch up with Rufus jist like hit did with Burl.

Anyways, we has a new postman fer now, which is a woman. I'se never seed a woman postman afore. I bet she has all her toes. She hain't from Hogwaller and she's real offish acting. Jist today she brung the mail up to the door because I had ordered from the JC Penny catalogue and hit wouldn't fit into the box. She brangs hit to the door and says all polite like "Are you Clem Clodhopper?" in some sort of furriner drawl. Hit were English but hit sounded like she were from one of them countries whut lies over the oceans. Wal, I tells her yes I am Clem Clodhopper, and she hands me the package and looks about like she can't believe whut she's a'seein'. She asks me iffen I lives there alone, and I says yes because I hain't rude even though I didn't see whys she would need to know. Hit's all very strange and hit will be interesting to see how folks hereabouts will take to her. Wal, I need to keep hit short today. Paw wants me to holp out down at the mayor's office and later I'se going to go holp with the drilling fer water on Paw's property. My GED test will be back soon, and I will write and lets you know how it went.

Until then, I am Clem Clodhopper, high school graduate (I hopes).

Respectively,

Clem

News From the GED Testing Center

December 27, 2002

GED Testing Centeer
1201 Turner Street
Little Rock, Arkansas

Mr. Clem Clodhopper
Rural Route 1
Hogwallow, Arkansas

Dear Mr. Clodhopper:

We wish you the best during this holiday season and hope you and your family have had a very merry Christmas. We know you have been anxiously awaiting the results of the GED testing you recently completed. We here at the GED Testing Center try to get results back to our clients as quickly as possible. However, with that said, I am afraid we have run into some complications in grading your exam. Let me be more succinct by putting this into a list of problems we found on your test sheet.

First, there was a problem with stray marks on the exam answer sheet. The instructions were to mark only the spaces provided for the answers as any stray marks might skew the results. The joke that you told about the possum was indeed funny. It had Mrs. Eidelmann in hysterics as she is a New Yorker and can envision herself dressing a possum. However, to put it on the test answer sheet has caused our grading machine to jam, and it took two professionals working three hours to get it operational again. In addition, while we appreciate the art work of the cows, and trees, and flowers, etc., it, too, further hindered our efforts to grade the test. Might we suggest that you not attend art school or make art your major should you choose to attend a university.

Secondly, it is not allowable for clients to put in answers other than those given. Although you might feel that your answer is better, you must choose one of the selections offered. Although you did eventually pick one of our answers, to write in what you thought it should have been jams our machines. See the previous paragraph.

Thirdly, While the essay on your mother was heartwarming and very emotional, we have one suggestion for further essays you might have to do. First, stick to the subject and, secondly, do not do so much recapping of events as the essay progresses. For example, you were telling of your mother's ability to capture catfish using just her hands, and then you digressed to Buddy Carmack's unfortunate demise from salmonella after eating a five day old catfish fillet. That story line alone took up half your essay and really had nothing to do with your mother's ability to catch fish. In addition, each time a name was mentioned in your essay, if it appeared a second time later in the essay, you recapped or summarized what you had said about that person previously, which makes for redundancy and detracts from the flow of the essay.

With all that having been said, we decided to grade the test by hand and award you your correct answers. We would not normally do this as a matter of course. But we felt there were some unusual circumstances at play in this case. In addition, it came to our attention that Evanell Plumlee was your tutor in preparing for the exam, and her father is one of the biggest donors to the GED testing centers in Arkansas. We would not want to upset Ms. Plumlee and thereby cause her to talk to her father about withdrawing his support. So we took the higher ground and decided to let your test grade stand on its own merits. Your score was a 75 and you have passed your GED exam. Congratulations, Mr. Clodhopper. You are now ready to apply to the university of your choice. We would like to end by wishing you and your family the very best of New Years.

Sincerely yours,

Geoffrey Spurgeon,
Testing Coordinator

Delivering the Mail

January 2, 2003

Dear Miss Amelia,

A happy new year to you. I know that in New York they has a real wing ding to celebrate New Year whut with that big ball a'droppin' down and all. Here in Hogwaller we keeps it simpler. Jess Mosier jist climbs up into the church steeple and when we yells up, "Jess, hit's midnight," he whangs that bell with a big old sledge hammer and we all starts to hoo rahing. Of course, hit's days afore Jess gits his hearing back, but we thank hit's a small price to pay fer celebrating a new year. We's jist glad this year warn't like the last when Jess had jist a mite too much to drank and clanged that bell. Them vibrations nearly knocked him out of the steeple whut with him being a little unsteady and all. Anyways, I hope you had a good Christmas and a good New Years.

Wal, I has done hit. I am a high school graduate. My test scores are back and I gots a 75, which is purty good. Them GED folks was awful nice and made some helpsome comments about whut to do on other tests. I'm not shore about iffen they liked my stories and jokes or not. City folk don't have time to git a sense of humor I reckon. Anyways, I passed and to celebrate, Maw cooked up a big skillet of sweet taters and some pork chops and corn pone which is only my favorite meal. Throw in some good, cold buttermilk and hit's a meal you won't soon fergit. I stopped by to give the Widow Plumlee a big plate full the next day and she were most grateful. I thanked her for holping me to pass the test, and she says not to be a stranger. She thanks that I could still learn a lot from her and mebbe I should come by a couple of times a week jist to brush up on my talking and writing lessons. I shakes her hand and hugs her real big, and she gits all flustered and turns real red. Why, you could cook an aig on her face. I'm not shore why that woman is so fidgety around me, but she is in a nervous tick most of the time I'm around.

The removal of the Poindexter house has gone real quick. With all his boys, Burl had a ready made crew all raring to go. And to make hit even better, several famblys came by to holp. I guess they's looking forward to gitting some clean dranking water. Delilah has been drapping by a couple of times a week and leaving some of her cookies and candies. Maw ain't really happy about Delilah after the way she done me at the alter, but you knows Maw. She hain't going to turn anyone away, even Delilah. She says she has tried to forgive Delilah but hit hain't been easy. A maw's love for her son is somethang you don't want to mess with.

Git this. You remembers whut I tolt you about Jake losing his job fer a'carryin' whiskey to customers for Rufus Sweeney and a'gittin' caught when ol' Miss Henry who is a teetotaler fount a pint in her mail and turned hit in and Jake were fired and they gots a woman to delivery the mail who is a furriner? Wal, don't you know Rufus has been arrested jist days after Jake got caught. Hit seems that Rufus asked the new mail lady to do the same thing whut Jake was a'doin' which were a big mistake. Hit turns out she is a'workin' for the FBI and was sent to find out who was a'usin' the mail to carry whiskey. Now, Rufus made a bunch of mistakes. First, he didn't take time to really git to know her. Her furriner way of talking should have told him she warn't from around here and you don't trust furriners. No offense, Miss Amelia. Yore an exception. Second, she is a woman and most wimmen can't be trusted. No offense, Miss Amelia. Yore an exception agin. I'm a'talkin' about wimmen like Delilah and furriner wimmen. Third, she asked a lot of questions and you can't trust wimmen and furriners and people who are wimmen and furriners and askes a lot of questions. So she arrestes Rufus and takes him to jail. Hit couldn't have happened to a nicer feller. Maw says God gits you in the end and God got Rufus's end real good.

Paw says that iffen the drilling folks hain't struck water in the next few days, he's a'goin' to give up on the well. Hit stinks something terrible there where's they is working and since Shankey Branch Crik will be clean, he don't want to spend any more money on a well. That plot of land is jist worthless for anythang, I reckon.

I'm guessing yore trip to Hogwaller is a'comin' up real soon. We'uns is looking forward to yore visit. Maw has got everythang as clean as hit can be. Paw says you can eat offen the floors. And we has done that afore when the floor warn't near as clean. Delilah is working up one of them proposals to give you whut would make you and yore

107

Designin' Wimmen partners in her cookie and candy business. Brother Johnson is working up a whole passel of new sermons so's you can hear how good he talks. The Widow Plumlee is adding some new books to the liberry. Hit seems fer some strange reason that the GED folks has sent her a bunch of books fer the liberry which has about doubled whut hit was. They's real nice folks, them GED people. And I'm jist a'chompin' at the bit to take you to them dances and shows you whut a good dancer I am. You remembers Fred Astair and Gene Kelso and them old timey dancers? Wal, they hain't got nothing on me. Paw says I'se got natural rhyme and I gits hit from him. He don't dance much anymore because Maw can't move around too good, and she don't want him dancing with other wimmen. She's a tad jealous. Hit's her only real flaw.

Wal, I'm a'goin' to back out of here and git some vittles. Hit's my birthday tomorry and Maw is planning a big wing ding of a meal fer me. She says I can have whatever I likes sense hit's my birthday. Being as I've had corn pone and sweet taters and pork chops jist the tother day, I thank I'm going fer a big steak and greens with a big mater and I'm going to stick with that sweet tater. Them's my favorites. I won't say how old I'se going to be, but Paw says you're only as old as you feels young. That Paw is a real philanderer. He has a saying for everythang. Have a good day, Miss Amelia. I'se looking forward to seeing you. You almost seem like fambly in a way.

Yore birthday boy,

Clem

Amelia's Impending Trip

January 12, 2003

Dear Clem,

I was so elated to hear of your good news To think that you have worked for and accomplished something so important to you makes me very happy. Now that you don't have to worry about the GED, I can come to Hogwallow and know I won't be a distraction in your pursuit of that lofty goal. I believe I am arriving at an opportune time to get material for my magazine. It seems that something momentous is always happening there. How exciting to live in such a place! If things go as I have planned them, I should be arriving there in one week from today. I do wish I could have been there in time for your birthday. I know that it was quite a celebration. Mine is coming up soon, and I am not looking forward to it at all. But that's still a little while away so I am going to enjoy the age I am now for just a bit longer. For now, my ticket is set and since you have taken care of my accommodations there, it seems I have nothing to be concerned about except the anticipation of meeting so many people about whom I have only read. I will try to conduct my research as inconspicuously as I can while still trying to be a part of the social life there. I am anxious to meet your family and the Poindexters and all the other denizens of Hogwallow.

I was so sorry to hear about Jake and his tribulations. Now that the FBI agent has got her man, perhaps Jake will be allowed to go back to his job. Since Bill Clinton is my second cousin, I could appeal to him to help Jake. He is a good man in spite of that Lewinsky woman. Delivering the mail is a very important responsibility. How well I remember an encounter with a postal worker that left me in tears. I had just received a note informing me that I had been sent a package of Ralph Lauren products, and I was to pick it up at the post office because it had to be signed for me to receive it. I rushed right over because it contained perfumes and cosmetics that I had been eagerly awaiting. Well, the clerk was so rude. She made me show her some identification and two credit cards and a driver's license. I was so embarrassed. My picture on my driver's license is horrendous. I was so mortified by all the commotion. They should have known who I was. Did they think I was a terrorist, for heaven's sake? Well, I picked up my package and I rushed right out of there. You have no idea how hard it is to live here in New York. Your small hamlet must be an Eden in comparison.

It seems that you have everything well prepared for my arrival. Pastor Johnson and Ms. Plumlee and even the Poindexters will be wonderful I know. How kind of them to take me in. And, of course, your mother and father will be their kind selves as always. Yes, I am looking forward so much to going to dances with you. I do love to dance. I can see us there under the stars with the band softly playing and the two of us dancing in rhythm as the music wafts softly into the night air. Our bodies will be as one, rhythmically undulating against each other as you crush me to your chest. I will feel the heat from your body as you pull me to you in cadence to the beat and the pulse of the…Oh, my! What am I saying? I think I have the vapors. I must get a cold cloth for my head…

There now. I feel much better. I must quit reading those romance novels. Oh, you must think me so wanton to speak in such a way to you. Perhaps we should not do the slow dances. My mother has never let me do slow dances as she feels they lead to improper behavior and I am sure she is right. I must be going now. For some reason after I write a letter to you I feel the need to take a cold bath which I will do before I retire. I look forward to our first meeting and I wish you well until then.

Affectionately,

Amelia.

Amelia Meets the Clodhoppers

January 23, 2003

Amelia Winslow Blythe
Rural Route 1
Hogwallow, Arkansas

Anne and Jack Blythe
1326 Valley View Road
Raleigh, North Carolina

Dear Mother and Father,

Well, I have finally arrived. If not socially, and least geographically. I am in Hogwallow, Arkansas. You remember I told you that I would be doing a story for my magazine about the culture of the rural mountain families of Arkansas and that I would be staying with my friend Clem whom I met through correspondence and who has provided me families with whom to stay while I am here. The first week is with Clem's family, and I can see that it will be an experience that I won't soon forget and an excellent opening segment for my article. Clem is a rural bumpkin and a real diamond in the rough. He is a little over six feet tall and weighs about 190 pounds. He has a mighty mouse chest, dark hair, and lovely dark brown eyes. But the most infectious and endearing part of his personality is his smile and his genuine likeability. For having never gone to a formal school, he is very intelligent, charismatic and utterly charming in a rustic way. He has a ready wit that belies the stereotypes that we associate with the hillbilly culture. He met me at the airport in Little Rock and drove me the hundred miles to Hogwallow in a car that would have frightened the Beverly Hillbillies. He talked nonstop all the way to his parents' house, and I feel that I know more about his life than anyone other than his mother and father. I did manage to get in a few comments and questions which he answered at length, often giving an anecdote to make his point. Some of his tales you would think are too improbable to be believed. But I really do feel they are true stories based on what he has written in his letters.

Clara May Clodhopper, Clem's mother, is just lovely. Were she in another culture at another time, she could fit in with the highest of society. She is one of those women who, had her lot in life been different, would have been a Marie Curie, a Sojourner Truth, or Amelia Earhart. She has spunk, fortitude, resilience, and pride in herself and her family. She is honest, hardworking, and bears herself with decorum. When she is around the other women of the community, she stands as a swan among crows. She has been so kind to me already, and it is evident that she has gone to great lengths to impress me in her housewifery skills. In the two days I have been here, I have already grown quite fond of her, and I do think she likes me. The week here will go too quickly, and I will be hesitant to move on to my new family at week's end. Clem comes by often, and the good natured banter between Clem and Clara May reveals a deep and abiding affection for each other.

Clayton Clodhopper has impressed me greatly in a short time. I can see Clem in him, and that is not a bad thing because he is a handsome man. He is in his late fifties and very youngish looking for his age. He has worked hard all his life and has been a faithful husband and a good father. He worships Clem and admits he has spoiled him after losing his other son at such a young age. He likes to wear overalls and, while that may seem like a stereotype, they look good on him. His clothes are always clean and his shirts pressed because Clara May won't let him go into town to perform his duties as mayor looking like a roughneck. She feels Clayton's appearance is a reflection on her and her household. He welcomed me like a member of the family. I have already gotten a veritable book of homilies from him as he views himself as quite the philosopher. He has some adage for every occasion and, after talking to him for a great length of time, it is easy to see where Clem gets his wit.

The first night with the Clodhopper family, Clem stayed later than usual before he went to his own home. We all had dinner together. They refer to their food as "vittles" which has a common, folksy ring to it. Clara May had prepared an elegant meal of chicken, potatoes, turnip greens, and corn bread. True, it was country fare and prepared in the country tradition, but it was delicious. It is what I refer to as "comfort" food. I watched her as she prepared the meal and complimented her on her culinary skills, which made her blush and pleased her to no end. It was not a hollow compliment because she is a very good chef in her own way.

After the meal, we retired to the front porch to sit and talk and listen to the night sounds of the local "critters" as they serenaded us. While we sat and softly talked, I observed the most fascinating thing. There was an abundance of fireflies, and they lit up the night with synchronized flashes. It was a synchronization unlike anything I have ever seen. It was a precision to make a concert master proud, and it continued for some time while we sat and marveled. At least I marveled because I had never seen anything like it living with all the lights in New York City. The air was clean with only the slightest hint of wood smoke occasionally wafting upon the air and the subtle odor coming from Clayton's pipe when he lit it. Clem is a good hand with a guitar, and no sooner had he played a lovely tune upon it than three other neighboring men brought their instruments over and joined in. I have not gone to a lovelier concert in the symphony halls in New York. It was indeed a wonderful night and one I will remember when I get back to the boring routine of everyday life in New York.

Tomorrow is Sunday and we will all be going to church together. I asked Clara May if she would wear the hat and scarf that Clem had written me about and she agreed to do so. Her hair has grown back out and is a beautiful shade of brown, and I made sure to compliment her on how nice it looked. She was most pleased since Clem and Clayton pay little attention to such things, being typical men. I will get to meet some of the families with whom I will be staying and will hear Brother Johnson give one of the sermons he has prepared because he knew I would be coming to hear him. I guess it will be nice for the other members to hear something new instead of a rehashing of old sermons. It will be an interesting day, and I am looking forward to it. I am filling a lot of pages in my journal, and I believe the magazine will be pleased with what I am discovering about these families who are isolated from the world, yet seem the happier for it.

Now I must retire because everyone here is in bed no later than nine o'clock. It would be rude on my part to be up and stirring around while everyone else is trying to sleep. I will get more sleep while I am here than I am accustomed to getting with the distractions that New York offers. Here, once dinner is done and the social part that follows, then it's to bed until Clara May starts breakfast the next morning. Believe me, Mother, I never got up this early for one of your meals. I do not mean that in a bad way. It's just that they expect you to arise when they do in the Clodhopper household. I will write again very soon as things will be happening very quickly I know.

With great affection,

Amelia

Delilah Gets Saved

January 27, 2003

Amelia Winslow Blythe
Rural Route 1
Hogwallow, Arkansas

Anne and Jack Blythe
1326 Valley View Road
Raleigh, North Carolina

Dear Mother and Father,

I'm in my second week and am now staying at the Johnson's home. You remember Brother Johnson who is the minister at the First Footwashing Baptist Church of the Second Coming of Hogwallow who was to officiate at Cecil's wedding but had a coronary and a substitute minister had to perform the ceremony. Well, I'm now at his home and what a change this has been for me.

First, let me tell you about my last days at the Clodhopper's. In my last letter to you I had been in the Clodhopper household for two days, and they were the most interesting people you could ever meet. I gave a glowing report of their hospitality in my last missive to you and as the week progressed, it only got better. More gracious and attentive hosts could not be found at the finest hotels in America. Early in my stay there, Mrs. Clodhopper would not let me do anything as far as household chores, but as the week progressed, she graciously let me take a small part in the cooking, and many dishes that I made I had to substitute items because they would not have what I needed since her larder simply was not set up for gourmet cooking. Yet, whatever I made, the whole family praised to the skies and said they had never tasted anything like it. I wasn't sure if it were meant in a complimentary way or not, but it had to be as they would never say anything to make anyone feel uncomfortable. Most nights we stayed up past their bedtimes because they wanted to know as much about my

115

world as I did about theirs.

At night it was a serenade from nature as we sat on the porch or a symphony from Clem and the neighbors as they played and sang. What a beautiful, simplistic life they live. They are honest and hardworking for the most part. Of course, there are some here, as there are everywhere, who will try to get something for nothing, but the majority are people who would be admired in any society for their integrity. Clem's family is a perfect example. I would go as far as to say that despite our divergent backgrounds, I would not hesitate to be Clem's date at the biggest social functions in New York. I know that his simple, trusting nature would get him through in any situation. He has already taken me to one social function here. On Saturday nights, there is a square dance at the local town hall, and Clem and a few friends perform the music for the dances. When he was not playing, we danced and, though I am not very good at the square dance form, Clem made it seem effortless when we dosie doed. I don't think any of my stays in the other households will compare to the Clodhopper's, but I will keep an open mind.

The Johnson's are a real interesting study. Mr. Johnson, as I mentioned earlier, is the minister here in Hogwallow and has been for some twenty-five years. The congregation seems to know his sermons by heart, and many have told me that my coming must have inspired him, for his recent efforts have been fresh and interesting. I only wish that he would save his sermons for the church, but he seems to like to hear himself talk at home also. During dinners, it is hard to get a real conversation going because he monopolizes most of what is being discussed. As I was there to learn, I guess I shouldn't be upset since I was getting information about the people there, but it was so refreshing at the Clodhopper's to be asked about my life and know they were genuinely interested. Brother Johnson spent a lot of time talking about his physical ailments and how the Lord had helped him to overcome them, such as the coronary, which Clem called a corona, bless his heart.

The one interesting thing that happened that is really noteworthy is a baptism that Brother Johnson performed. It was none other than Delilah Poindexter. Delilah has been a steady visitor to the Clodhopper household and now the Johnson household since I have been here. I am sure she is trying to make an impression on me with her cookie and candy business, but the impression she made did not stem from her baking skills. Delilah, as I have written you, is the woman who jilted Clem on his wedding day. I will have to admit that she is a beautiful woman, and, despite her obvious social deficiencies, would be a striking figure in most walks of life based on her physical beauty alone. Though she is a frequent visitor to the Clodhopper's, Clem seems to take it as a matter of course. I think he has moved past Delilah, and whatever charm she had woven around him does not exist now. He is so good that way. He takes what life gives him and faces the bad with aplomb and dignity. Delilah seems to know that, but her vanity keeps her from admitting it to herself. However, one Sunday Delilah surprised everyone, especially her family. When Brother Johnson called for those who wanted to be saved to come forward, Delilah stood and walked proud and fearlessly to the front of the church. Burl, who sleeps through most of the sermon, was nudged awake by Jethro and nearly choked on the chew of tobacco he had concealed in his gum. Delilah confessed her sins to the church and did it in such a beautiful and dignified way that it brought tears to my eyes. She even apologized to the Clodhopper family and especially to Clem for all that they suffered because of her own thoughtlessness and selfishness. But she especially wanted to be a good mother and role model to her child, and she wanted to start by being baptized into the church. But get this. It was Clovis who did the baptism. Here is Clovis, this good-natured bear of a man who had once pelted Annabelle with tomatoes and who is the brother to Delilah, performing her baptism. Since Clovis had been studying to be a minister, Brother Johnson thought this would be a major step in that direction. Nothing could have been more dramatic or ironic or endearing. And as Brother Johnson held her child, Clovis dipped Delilah into the water, and even Burl had to wipe a tear from his eye, though he pretended it was simply the effects of the tobacco juice he had swallowed.

Tomorrow, I will be moving into the Widow Plumlee's house, and I am looking forward to that. Of all the people here, she seems to be the most intellectually stimulating. I am sure that we will be able to discuss many subjects together since she is so well versed in so many areas of academia. She is also very close to my age, so we will have a lot in common in that respect. I will write again in a few days and let you know how things are progressing.

I see Clem almost every day. I think he likes me but he is not pushy in that regard, and I am just going to let things take their course.

Until I talk to you again, I will keep you in my thoughts.

With deep affection,

Your daughter Amelia

The Widow Plumlee

February 1, 2003

Amelia Winslow Blythe
Rural Route 1
Hogwallow, Arkansas

Anne Blythe
1326 Valley View Road
Raleigh, North Carolina

Dear Mom,

I wrote this letter to you, and it is intended for your eyes only as I know Dad would have a hard time with it. This is girl talk and you have always been good to be honest with me when it comes to matters of the heart.

I started this letter strangely I know, but many things have come to the surface since I have begun my stay at the Widow Plumlee's home. First, let me say she is a lovely person in physical appearance and in spirit. She lost her husband in an unusual way and after only a short time of being married. She comes from a influential and well-to-do family. How she wound up here in Hogwallow was one of my first questions. She said that a woman should follow her husband and support him in whatever vocation and whatever location he chose. Her husband was an agricultural extension agent, and he was sent to Hogwallow to be of assistance to the local farmers, primarily to help them produce better crops through more scientific agricultural methods, thereby hopefully reducing the number of needy families and families on welfare in the area. From Mrs. Plumlee's description of her husband, he was an intelligent and personable man and respected by most of the residents of Hogwallow and Hootin' Holler. However, he was warned that he had to be careful while going from place to place in the hills of these tiny communities as there were many moonshiners and marijuana growers who would shoot first and ask questions later.

119

There is still quite a lawless element in these small towns in the backwoods of Arkansas. Tim, her husband, did well and won the respect of the locals, but he too often stepped on the toes of the wrong people.

Tim left for work on one Monday morning and did not return. When he did not return home the second day, Evanell went to Sheriff Tate and reported him missing. A search party was formed and late in the day, just before nightfall, one of the dogs sniffed out his body which was lying propped against a tree, and a bottle of moonshine lay by his outstretched hand. It seems that he had gotten a bad bottle of liquor and had died of moonshine poisoning. Evanell could not understand how it could have happened. She never knew her husband to drink in all the years she had known him. This would be totally out of character. Sheriff Tate commented that we often don't know the people we marry. Still, Evanell would not be convinced that this was not foul play. Someone had forced him to drink the whiskey and that someone had known that it would poison him. That someone was probably one of the local moonshiners whom Tim had unfortunately stumbled upon in his daily treks to different farms. The mystery of his death is still unsolved, and Evanell feels it won't be in such a backward community with few resources to call upon in solving homicide cases. It was put into a file and lies buried under other papers in the sheriff's office until it can be looked into more thoroughly, which Evanell feels will be never.

Such a tragedy to happen to someone so young and so in love. And that brings me to the second surprise I got from Evanell. She thinks she is in love with Clem. As you can understand, this creates a problem for me as I have grown to respect and admire him so much myself. I am not saying that I am in love with him, but that is not to say it could not happen in the future. So you can see how difficult this would be for me to discuss with Evanell. She told me of the nights they spent together preparing him for the GED and how difficult it was to concentrate on the subject matter when he was so close. She told of how many times they would make incidental contact and how she would get short of breath and her body would tremble, and she just knew that Clem noticed. This embarrassed her to no end. She is such a fragile and docile thing, like a frightened doe almost, and she would never be able to tell Clem how she felt. But get this. She wants me to be a go-between and plead her case to Clem for her. I never fancied myself a John Alden, and I especially do not want to do so in this case as I have gotten to know Clem and would like to see where our relationship goes.

Just the other night after a walk along the river, Clem took my hand to help me over some fallen limbs, and for a second our bodies were almost touching. I looked up into his face and he spoke my name. It was almost as if he wished to say something important, and I moved closer and turned my lips upward to meet his when two of Burl Poindexter's boys happened by. We quickly separated and they walked by, snickering to each other and whispering. I knew what they were thinking and I know it embarrassed Clem. I hope this is not a set-back in our relationship. We were so close for just a second, and I believe he has feelings for me and can't express them, much the same as in Evanell's case.

So, Mother, what do I do? Be my Dear Abby and tell me what you would do in this situation. I do not want to hurt Evanell who has already suffered so much. Yet, I do not want to push Clem to her and risk the chance of losing him in the process. You see why I could not let Father know. He would bluster and fume and talk about how a simple hillbilly would not be good enough for his daughter. Please do not say anything to him until I know where I stand in Clem's heart. Things are so complicated when it comes to affairs of the heart. I looked forward to hearing your sage advice on my dilemma. It will be good in a way to get on to my stay at the Poindexter's and get away from all of Evanell's histrionics. I hope to goodness Delilah does not tell me she still loves Clem and ask me to put them together again. That would be just too much. I love you, Mom.

Affectionately,

Your daughter Amelia

Motherly Advice

February 10, 2003

Anne Blythe
1326 Valley View Road
Raleigh, North Carolina

Amelia Winslow Blythe
Rural Route 1
Hogwallow, Arkansas

Dear Amelia,

I am your mother and what I am now about to tell you is done with only the best of intentions. How can I possibly believe that you are in a town called Hogwallow and in Arkansas of all places! Why would you possibly want to go there even for a magazine article? Are there not places on the Riviera or in Barcelona or in the Bahamas to do stories? I can't imagine a daughter of mine living in the conditions to which you must be subjecting yourself. As your mother, I demand that you return to New York immediately and forget this country bumpkin that you think has captured your heart. To communicate with him from New York is one thing because then you do not have to live in filth and squalor and be without clean sheets and towels and hot baths, but to actually go there, knowing of the horrid conditions you will face, borders on the absurd. How will you get manicures and your beautiful hair styled properly? You must come home to me, for I feel that you have taken leave of your senses. You were always such a practical and refined young lady. Now you have become Daisy May chasing Li'l Abner through the hills of Dogpatch. I just do not understand you at all. Perhaps this young man does have some redeeming features. Maybe he bathes and wears clean clothes and has a smattering of manners. But, dear Amelia, please understand that beneath that veneer is a pure hayseed and no match in culture, social standing, or education with you.

You have asked me for guidance in this time of what I consider a major crisis in your life. I can only say that from your correspondence, I can see changes in you and none of them for the better. My goodness, you have even lost your ability to communicate using the lovely English you were taught. To think that we spent good money at a prestigious boarding school just to have you start an anecdote with "Now get this." And then to run on and on in sentences with no thought to a period is quite distressing to one who loves to see the written word done well. You are a Blythe at heart, and I know you will overcome whatever form of enchantment this Clem has cast over you. Let the Widow Plumlee and this Delilah woman have him and good riddance. I know this is not what you wanted to hear from me because you are thinking and acting with your heart and not your head. I would hate to consider what this Clem fellow is leading you into with his country charm. I know you are approaching thirty, and it is bothering you that you have not settled into a stable relationship with a nice young man, but give it more time. I can wait for a grandchild a little longer. Amelia Clodhopper does not have a ring that will get you invited into the social graces of the elite in New York.

Please take into serious consideration all that I have said and look at the impossibilities of forming a romantic alliance with a poor hillbilly. I do not think I am being culturally biased in this respect but simply being practical. I look forward to receiving your next letter which will tell me that you will either be going back to New York or you will be coming here for further instruction on what to do with your life. I miss you.

Your Mother

The Poindexters

February 15, 2003

Amelia Winslow Blythe
Rural Route 1
Hogwallow, Arkansas

Anne Blythe
1326 Valley View Road
Raleigh, North Carolina

Dear Mother,

I know that when I write you for advice, I will get an honest opinion. It may not be what I want to hear, but it will be how you feel. I do understand what you're saying and that you do feel very strongly that you are right. However, since you do not know Clem nor his family, you do not have a basis for an honest appraisal of the situation. Not everyone can be pigeonholed because of their social status or educational achievements. Clem and his family are some of those people. It is evident from your letter you still would like to control my life. I do not want to hurt your feelings, but I am almost thirty years old and I should know if what I feel for someone is love. My respect and love for you will never change, but I will have to go my own way on this. I guess what I was needing was validation, and you did not give me what I wanted to hear. You have always been honest in your feelings, and I should not expect anything different now. I know there is a good chance that Clem feels the same way about me, so there might come a time when how you perceive people based solely on their culture and social standing will become an issue between us. I hope it is not insurmountable.

Perhaps more of interest to you will be what I am experiencing with my new family. This week I am finishing my stay with the Poindexter's. In my first three weeks with three different families, I have gotten a broad spectrum of beliefs, values, personalities, work ethics, and an abundance of strange stories to record in my journal. With Burl and his children, I never know what to expect or how to prepare for it, so I simply take it as it comes. My stay with the Poindexters is nearly over and it's been an adventure unlike anything I have experienced. Here are some examples.

First, let me tell you about Burl, the father of the brood. I have written you about some of the activities of the family and their standing in the community. Burl has nine sons, a daughter, and a grandchild living in one house with him. If not for Delilah being here, it would be utter chaos and I would leave immediately. Burl chews tobacco, drinks too much, belches, is given to flatulence, picks his nose (which is utterly disgusting), and these are his good points. I'm sure somewhere under all that thick skin is a heart and soul, but I will have a hard time finding it. In his defense, he tries to be somewhat discreet when I am in the house, but his true nature usually wins out. Just yesterday, Delilah and I had made a very sumptuous meal and had set a nice table with a cloth and candles and had created a very nice atmosphere conducive to dining. Burl and the boys came in from the fields all covered with dirt and mud and plopped down without even bothering to change clothes. They did wash their faces and hands which is to their credit. During the meal, it was like refereeing a free-for-all at a pig sty. I had to check Delilah's baby on occasion just to be sure she didn't get eaten in the confusion. Clovis did say a prayer before the meal and Delilah tried to keep control as the meal progressed, but it was like trying to slow down a runaway train with your bare hands. It took Delilah and me working steadily an hour to clean up the kitchen once the meal was over.

Luckily, after the meal I do have a small house to retire to and be away from the mayhem at night. Delilah and the baby stay with me in the smaller house so I do have some company, and she makes sure I do not have to worry about the boys trying to sneak peeks at me when I am undressing to bathe or sleep. It's a far cry from the nights spent on the Clodhopper front porch listening to the night sounds or to Clem and his friends playing on their musical instruments. I know I will look back on the experiences with each of these families and take away some pleasant memories. With the Poindexters, I'm not sure what they are going to be. I miss Clem very much. While I have been staying with the Poindexters, he has not come to visit with me. It has only been a week, but it seems like two years. Of course, I knew this would be the case. Too much has happened between Clem's father and Burl for Clem to ever feel comfortable in the Poindexter household. I will have to make it a point tomorrow to get a message to Clem that I would like for him to take me to get some spices from the local mercantile. Yes, it is a simple ruse I will admit, but Clem will not recognize it as being anything of that nature. He is so trusting and helpful. I do believe that he is the dearest man that I have ever met.

This week has been a long one for me. Delilah is really delightful in a back woods kind of way. She wants to go to New York and start a business selling her candies and cookies, which are excellent, but she does not have the skills in marketing to make a success of it. I hesitate to tell her this because I do not want to squelch her dreams for a life outside of Hogwallow. If I could, I would become an advisor and guide in her endeavors, but this would put a burden on my own career which is just now showing fruition. There is so much she would have to learn and it would not be just business. Surviving in New York on a daily basis is difficult for someone as seasoned as I am. It would destroy a novice like Delilah. But she likes to talk about what she would do there and how her baby would have a better life. I listen but I do not offer encouragement that would lead her to believe that it would be a simple thing to accomplish. I do not think she knows how I feel about Clem which leads me to believe that when two of Burl's boys saw Clem and me at the riverbank that they did not say anything to her. I'm sure she is not privy to many things that go on in their lives as they do not talk to her very much. So she often breaks into a reverie talking about how she and Clem were once going to be married. She admitted that she had never truly loved Clem. She was only doing what her father had wanted her to do in order for him to get the land on which his house now sits. She regrets her actions so much and truly wishes she get Clem to believe that of her. The future I see for Delilah is not in New York or any other big city. Her fate, I believe, is to marry some local chap and live in these hills for the rest of her life. I do not mean to insinuate that it is a bad thing. I simply believe it is best for her and her child.

The child is beautiful. Her name is Annie and she has her mother's looks. She is such a quiet baby and coos and smiles and seems quite content most of the time. I think that even Burl likes her, being that there is finally a female child in the family. And for some strange reason she seems perfectly content when Burl picks her up like a sack of potatoes and carries her around singing some strange mountain song that Annie appears to like very much. I asked him to give me the words and he sang them to me. He has a beautiful voice that belies his personal characteristics, and I can see why little Annie would enjoy it. He says he made it up and he calls it "Annie's Lullaby."

> "Sleep, little Annie,
> Ready for bed.
> Upon the pillow,
> Lay your sweet hand "

> "Wee, precious bundle,
> Wrapped up so tight;
> Pray softly slumber
> All through the night."

> "Sleep, little Annie;
> Day is nigh done.
> Sleep, little angel,
> 'Til morrow dawns."

Burl sat by Annie's crib tonight and sang until she went to sleep. It's that type of thing that makes me believe there's more to the man than the outward appearance and actions. It just reinforces my belief that all that glitters is not gold, and gold doesn't necessarily have to glitter. I see gold in Clem. Perhaps you will have an opportunity to see it for yourself. Well, Burl has gone home and I'm feeling a little sleepy myself after hearing Annie's lullaby. I'll write again before I go home to New York. I'm sure much will have happened by then.

Your loving daughter,

Amelia

Amelia Returns Home

February 20, 2003

Amelia Winslow Blythe
Designing Women
Trump Towers
New York, New York

Anne and Jack Blythe
1326 Valley View Road
Raleigh, North Carolina

Dear Mom and Dad,

This morning at 10:30 I left Hogwallow to return home. I am now back in New York, and I just had to sit down and give you all the news of my last days there. Clem took me to the airport in Little Rock, and we talked all the way and parted with great sadness. I will go into several reasons why the departure was so sad for us later in the letter. Clem had to leave me sooner than he would have wished because news had been brought to him that something was happening on the scrub acreage where his father had been drilling for water. You remember that Clem's father had been cheated out of his land by Delilah and Burl when Delilah left Clem at the altar, and Burl would not give back the land he had gained under false pretenses from the Clodhoppers. I suppose to salve his own conscience, Burl had given Mr. Clodhopper several acres of scrub property which wasn't any good because it was bog-like and had an awful smell. Mr. Clodhopper had been drilling for water on it for some time. I suppose they found it because Mr. Clodhopper told Clem to return quickly from the trip to Little Rock and go directly to the property to help the men working there. I was not unhappy to get out of the Poindexter household, though I did gain a lot of knowledge about the area from Burl who knew the hills probably better than anyone because he had been one of the biggest moonshiners in that area many years ago. A lot of the lore and legend I have for my book ironically came from Burl who is quite the historian when it comes to this little section of Arkansas. He knew of all the families who had ever lived there, all their stories in great detail, and he had an amazing memory for names of family members. After dinner, most nights would be spent with me talking to Burl and extracting from him some of the most amazing nuggets of journalistic gold. He and his boys were not nearly as bad as I thought they would be in their treatment of me.

I believe Delilah helped out in that area. She told me of the one great tragedy in their lives when Josephine Poindexter died giving birth to Jethro. Burl won't talk about it, but Delilah filled me in on the details. At least now I understand a little more of why Burl has become so sullen and obstinate and so slovenly in his habits and manners. He lost a very important part of his life when he lost Josephine.

I have some news which may or may not be what you want to hear. I left Hogwallow with a heavy heart. I told you of my feelings for Clem and how I thought he felt the same way about me. Two nights before I was to come home, Clem and I made again the walk along the river and talked. On our previous walk we had been interrupted by two of Burl's boys just when I thought Clem was going to kiss me. This time there were no interruptions, and Clem told me how he had come to care a great deal for me. He had gotten a hint of how I felt through our correspondence and, after spending many days with me, he had come to feel the same. That night on the river bank he drew me into his strong arms and kissed me so passionately that I was surprised by its intensity. He is so easy going and shy in so many ways. Yet there was a sense of urgency almost in the way he held me, and he was hesitant to let go of my hand even for a moment. I felt a sense of exhilaration that I have not felt in years. Still, even with the happiness we were feeling, I could see apprehension in his face. When I asked him what was wrong, he looked away for a moment as if to collect his thoughts. Then he told me why he had been so hesitant to let his feelings be known. The crux of what he told me amounted to three major problems in his mind.

One was the obvious difference in our cultures. He knew he could never fit into my world, and he felt I would not be happy in his. Even though I assured him that I had never been happier than in the four weeks that I had been staying in Hogwallow, he argued that this feeling would pass and that I would eventually be unhappy there without the stimulation of the big city.

Another was the disparity in our education. I have a doctorate from one of the most prestigious schools in North Carolina, and he until recently had only a third grade education. Even with the GED, he knows he would never be my equal in what he calls "book learning."

And thirdly, and most importantly to him, is what he sees as his inability to support me if we were to get married. He has no job and no prospects. He knows that he could never respect himself if he could not provide for me. Even though I have assured him that if I had to take care of both of us I could do so, he would not listen to reason. He has his own code which I am sure has been instilled in him by his father. It is the man's job to provide for his family, and he won't have it any other way. Until he can do that, he cannot marry me. So, Mother, I know this news will make you happy, but it leaves me with a great sadness that weighs on me like a rock upon my heart. You and Father have such a great marriage and I know that Clem and I could have the same happiness, but the fates have played a cruel joke that apparently I must endure on my own. Clem is to write me soon with news of what the great uproar was all about with the drilling. Hopefully, he will also tell me that he has reconsidered and will marry me. This is my fervent hope, but I do not believe in my heart that I will receive such news. I am tired after my flight, and I must get some rest. I will write again soon.

Amelia

A Startling Discovery

February 25, 2003

Dear Miss Amelia,

Some purty exciting thangs have been a'happenin' since you done left to git back to New York. Later on in his letter, I will go into some detail. I thank whut you are going to hear will please you. I ain't one for purty words as you know, but I've been thanking a lot about you since you done flew back to New York. Hit's not quite the same here without yore womanly charms to brighten thangs up a mite.

Maw says that I needs to stop moping around and git to work so's I won't be thanking of you all the time. I went down to the river the other day, you know where's we were when we first kissed, and I sat there a tolerable time and thought about whut I could do so's we could be together. I ain't much on looks ner brains, but I got a strong back and a good sense of humor. I reckon a strong back ain't needed much in New York, and, iffen you lives there, you probably ain't got much of a sense of humor. Of course, yore an exception, Miss Amelia. I can't say all that my heart feels like them poets does, but I got a passel of thangs that I need fer you to know.

I like the way yore soft smile brightens my day like the morning sun coming over the hills here in the holler and how yore voice can git my heart to sanging like we did them nights out on the porch at Maw and Paw's. I can still see the golden yaller in yore hair as shiny and bright as the sunflowers out in Maw's garden. Them eyes of yorn are more sparkly than ary star in the night sky. Jist put all them thangs in a bundle and tie hit with a big red ribbon and hit's you, Miss Amelia. When a woman with looks and brains and yore cooking skills likes an old corn-fed boy from Arkansaw, he ort to let her know how he feels.

Miss Amelia, I hopes that being a criminal won't make me lesser in yore eyes. When I was a'comin' home from taking you to Little Rock, I got stopped by one of them Arkansaw State Troopers. Now I was in a hurry cause Paw done tolt me to git back home as quick as I could. My old truck ain't the fastest thang in the world, but I reckon I was a'goin' a tad over the speed limit as I didn't want to keep Paw waiting. Wal, this old boy turned them lights on and motioned fer me to pull over, which I did. He sidles up to the door like he was a'stalkin' a bear and says to give him my license. Whilst I'se gitting hit, he's a'lookin' my truck over like hit's one of them spaceships from Mars. He asked me where I had been and whut I had been a'doin'. Hit seems that some feller with a truck like mine had been running shine and he thought I was him. Wal, here in Arkansaw you can't go out of the house without falling over a moonshiner, so's I could see how he might have a problem gitting me mixed up with another feller. So with my good sense of humor, I thought I would make him laugh and show him that I ain't so bad.

I starts to telling him about Homer Ashlock who lives in Hootin' Holler and who has this old dog whut likes moonshine. Homer would always take Blue, that's Homer's dog, with him when he was making a run of moonshine. He treated Blue as good as any fambly member, mebbe better, knowing Homer's fambly. Wal, whenever Homer was waiting fer thangs to happen with the shine, he would sit down and take a nip to pass the time. Natural, he would give some to Blue since Blue were his only companion. Now old Blue developed a taste fer the stuff, don't you know, and Homer kept him well supplied. Usually, the shine would make Blue sleepy, and he'd jist curl up under a tree and sleep. But on this one day, he must of got a potent batch and decided he needed something to chase. Wal, he started with his tail, but he warn't making any headway ketching hit, so's he looked for somethang less vexing and seed a fox. He took off jist a'flyin' and a'howlin' and a'carryin' on. Natural, Homer figgered with all that noise somebody might come see whut the commotion was and find his still. He reckoned whut with Blue being drunk and all, he could jist run him down and take him home. Now git this pitcher. Here's the fox a'runnin' like all git out and Blue behind him staggering and stumbling and trying to ketch all three foxes that he's a'seein', and here comes Homer chasing after Blue to try and git him to the house so's his still won't be fount. They's all three a'runnin' through the woods, and the fox decides he is going to circle back, which is whut a fox will do to git rid of the dogs. Wal, he comes back jist a'whizzin' and darts through where the still is a'brewin' Homer's next run. Blue flies through and tips over the still, the mash, and all the makings that Homer had worked all day on. The place were a mess. Homer jist stopped and cussed the shine, the dog, the fox, and all his in-laws afore he took a breath. Old Blue and the fox ain't been fount yit. Homer decided that the day were ruint and he jist went home.

Homer didn't find out until two days later that them FBI boys had made a raid on several stills in them hills, and he would have been arrested iffen Blue hadn't got drunk and ruint his day's work. He reckons that Blue will come home when he gits his senses back.

So's I said to the Trooper, whut's the difference betwixt a drunk dog and a ugly Arkansaw State Trooper? Tomorry, the dog will be sober. Wal, that old boy jist looks at me like I'm crazy and askes me iffen I'm a'foolin' with him. Turns out he ain't only ugly but he ain't got no sense of humor nuther. He gives me this ticket, and I have to go all the way to Fayetteville to pay hit. Paw warn't too happy about me being a criminal, seeing that he's the mayor of Hogwaller. So's I reckon that's the bad news, but here's the good news. You remember all the ruckus that were a'goin' on when I left to take you to the airport in Little Rock? Hit seems that them old boys that Paw had drilling fer water out on his scrub property had run into some problems and called in some of them geolojists to check hit out. When them geolojist men gits there and checks out whut's going on, they gits real excited and starts to running back and forth and making calls on them cell phones, and all kinds of people in suits and with brief cases is suddenly appearing from everywhere. Them geolojists said that them smells whut had been coming from the place was because of sulfurous compounds which came from natural gas in the ground. Paw's scrub acres is a natural gas gold mine. A guy in a big fine suit tolt Paw that hit is part of the Fayetteville Formation Complex, and he said the find is a lot like the Barnett shale play in Oklahoma. Now me and Paw don't have no idee whut all that means. Turns out that we are a'sittin' on natural gas and a lot of hit. A man from the Southwestern Energy Company has offered Paw a lot of money to lease the mineral rights. They's going to spend millions of dollars gitting the gas out of the ground, and they said Paw is a wealthy man. I guess whut I'm a'sayin', Miss Amelia, is that I'm going to git a lot of money fer doing nothing. I knows hit won't make me smarter, and hit won't change where I come from, but hit will make gitting over those obstackles a lot easier. Paw's already got a big check and each month they will send him another'n fer as long as the fambly owns the land. Now, I won't have to worry about how I will support you iffen you'll have

133

me. I've got a lot of thangs to take care of here helping Paw sort through all them papers he has to sign. We got a lawyer out of Fayetteville to holp us. As soon as everythang is settled, I will write agin. Until then I will be thanking of you and hoping that you ain't changed yore mind about how you feel about me. I love you, Miss Amelia. And as that feller Shakeaspere said,

Oil's well that ends well,

Clem

Amelia in Love

March 7, 2003

Dear Clem,

I am elated to hear of your good fortune. This is a classic example of how riches will come to people who do the right thing. I can see Burl Poindexter's face now, and it is an angry face indeed. He tried to take advantage of you and your family, and now it has come back to haunt him. Knowing your father, he will put his good fortune to use not only to help his family but to improve the lives of all those in Hogwallow. Such a fortuitous circumstance could not have happened to a nicer and more deserving family. I won't bother to ask for too many details about how much money is involved because that is not for me to know since I am not family. I do hope, however, that it is enough to help with your schooling if you wish to pursue it. If the amount is substantial, will you be staying in Hogwallow or will you go out into the world to improve on your good fortune?

Clem, your last letter seemed to hint of a possible change of heart about our situation. I was never interested in whether you had money or not. Your education, or social standing, or financial status have never been factors in my feelings for you. You felt they were insurmountable and so I came back to New York. If your newly found fortune has caused you to reconsider, I am most willing to listen to any proposals you have in regard to our relationship. You know that I love you and nothing has changed that. You often say that you cannot express your feelings, but the sweet things you said in your letter were pure poetry and I will treasure them.

I was sorry to hear of your unfortunate run-in with the Arkansas State Trooper. I am afraid that law enforcement people in general have no sense of humor. I would have found your joke very humorous. Your receiving a ticket for speeding does not make you a criminal. I will get on the phone right now and call my cousin, who is former President Bill Clinton, and get that ticket taken off the books. The nerve of that state trooper to give you a ticket for simply obeying your

135

father's request to hurry home. He should have known that you weren't a moonshiner. You look nothing like the pictures of moonshiners that I have seen in magazines.

The editors of my magazine love the articles that I have written about your lovely town. My story will be featured in the next edition of *Designing Women Magazine* and then all the world will know about the good people of Hogwallow. Of course, your family is the main focus of the story, and it is an excellent human interest piece that I know will enthrall people and sell many magazines for my company. So if your natural gas strike did not make you famous, then my story will. I eagerly await more news on what will be going on with all the excitement of the gas strike on your property. If you would like me to come back to Hogwallow and help with the transition of the many changes that will happen to you, I will do so. And if you would like to come to New York and see the sights, and me, of course, I am agreeable to that also. Until I hear from you, I remain your Miss Amelia.

All my love,

Amelia

Amelia Gets a Surprise

March 16, 2003

Dear Miss Amelia,

I don't thank you git whut I am axbig fer you to do I want fer you to marry me now that I has become a wealthy man. So's you got to git back here as soon as you kin, and we will plan the biggest dang wedding this holler has ever seed. I knows that I am taking hit fer granted that you will say yes to my perposal of marriage, but I reckon yore last letter tolt me all I needed to know in that regard.

Maw is jist plain too excited to eat ner sleep since all these nice thangs have happened in the holler. Now that she knows I want to git married to you, she has plumb lost her mind with happiness. I reckon we can work out all the details when you git here. Thangs are a'happenin' faster than old Buford can shake his hind leg at these last few days. Natural, Burl is up in arms about the discovery of gas on the property that used to be his'n. So's he's hired Lawyer Bumpkus to take the case to see if he has a legal right to the property. Paw says Burl's jist spitting into the wind and nothing can come of hit. I knows Lawyer Bumpkus from another case that took place a few years ago in Hootin' Holler. Lawyer Bumpkus is the brother to Lester Bumpkus who if you remembers I tolt you about Lester gitting a new John Deere tracter whut is unusual in these parts because nobody I knows can afford hit and everyone figgered Lester had got it illegal like selling drugs. Wal, Lawyer Bumpkus seems to be cut from the same twist of baccer. Hit seems he likes them cases where the jury will award a bunch of money to a feller who gits done wrong like in a accident or if a customer spills hot coffee on hisself in a restaurant. Wal, I don't know about most people, but hit seems that iffen I ordered some coffee, I would expect hit to be hot. And iffen I'm dumb enough or clumsy enough to spill hit on myself, I expect I will git burned. So why would I sue somebody because I'se clumsy and stupid? I reckon there are a lot of folks in this world who have to blame other folks fer their problems.

Anyways, whut I was a'sayin' about Lawyer Bumpkus is that he ain't in it fer nothing but the money. In this one case, he was hired by Chester Sewell who lives in Hootin' Holler to sue Horace Dribble who lives in Hogwaller. Now these two old boys had been at hit fer some time. They's never gotten along and hits become almost as famous a feud as them Hatfields and McCoys. Chester will sneak over and let the air out of Horace's tracter tires, and Horace will hang a sign around the scarecrow in Chester's garden saying Chester eats snails. That kind of thang. Nothing but two men acting like kids. Then one day hit got serious. Horace sneaked over to Chester's house one day and put a burr under the saddle that Chester uses when he rides old Nellie, his horse. Chester goes out the next day and puts the saddle on Nellie, ignerant that there is a burr under the saddle. Wal, Chester climbs up into the saddle and when he sits down, that burr pierces old Nellie's hide and you ain't never seed a animal git so spirited. Now, you gots to understand that Nellie is about twenty years old, which is purty old fer a horse, but you wouldn't have knowed it by the way she were a'movin'. She were kicking her feet up in the air and spinning around afore she took off jist a'flyin' with Chester a'tryin' to hold on. She's a'goin' through bushes and limbs and briars and a'jumpin' fences, and Chester is gitting a mite scratched up until she decides to send him into the biggest briar patch in Hootin' Holler. Hit were a sight to see how Chester looked when he got hisself all excavated from them briars. The worsest of all is that he busted his right arm and had to git the doctor to set it. He accuses Horace of putting the burr under the saddle and sues him fer whut Bumpkus calls physical and mental anguish, whutever them thangs are. Bumpkus says that Chester can git several thousand dollars because he lost his ability to make a living whut with his arm being broke and all. Horace says he didn't do hit, and Chester can't prove hit nuther, so's they's going to trial and let a jury decide hit. I don't know which'un will win, but I'se got a feeling that the big winner will be Lawyer Bumpkus. I thank the jury ort to put him on Nellie and see how hit feels to be taken fer a ride. Anyways, he's the lawyer that Burl has hired, and Paw jist says you can always tell a lawyer but you can't tell him much. Paw has a saying fer about everything. He don't seem worried none, so I hain't going to worry about hit nuther.

Now here's the big news whut I was a'savin' fer last. The gas men from Southwestern Energy Company tolt Paw that he will be making

138

millions off the gas discovered on his property. Now I ain't good with figgers, but I thank that's a heap of money. I asked Paw to do me a favor fer a wedding gift to you. He agreed and we went to Fayetteville the other day and did some looking around fer whut I thought would please you the most and we bought hit. Hit's a restaurant, Miss Amelia. Hit's one of them high toned places whut cooks up them big city meals whut them highlanders like so much. They tolt me they even cook duck on a orange. They had some of the biggest craw fish I had ever seed, and poeple got to git up and look at them in this big tank and pick which they wanted. The manager took Paw and me in to look around in the dining hall and the kitchen, and everyone seemed real happy because they were a'smilin' and a'jostlin' each other as we walked around. They had them fancy waiters whut walked around in black suits and with towels on their arms and pouring champain and water and sich. One waiter even had another waiter who poured the water fer him. We went into the kitchen and Maw would have died. They had chefs all over the place, and they wore them big white hats and was jist slanging food everywheres. I ain't shore if I could survive on some of the food I saw on them plates. Why, they wasn't enough food on some of them to feed a baby. Jist a dab here and a dab there and some swirly stuff around the outside of the plate. I knows that none of them could cook like you can, so's I tolt Paw I wanted to buy the place and give hit to you as a wedding gift. You would be the owner and manager and main cook of the whole shooting match. Boy howdy! The meals you could cook up in that place. I even got a name for hit. I thank hit should be called Chef Amelia's. I only got one request and I thank you can do hit. There are a lot of fancy thangs on the menu, but I didn't see a thang for possum. Iffen you had possum on a stick or possum on a orange or possum on a bisket, I thank hit would sell like hotcakes. I'll leave hit up to you because hit will be all yores, but sense that is how we met, I thank hit would be right fitten and romanciful. You would still have time to make yore gadgetical thangs and write yore stories for Designin' Wimmen.

I shore hope you will let me do this fer you. Maw is a little upset about we might have to move to Fayetteville since she ain't used to the big city, but I tolt her she needs to stay in Hogwaller because her and Paw ain't never knowed nothing else and are too old to learn. We will be fine because you know big city ways, and I learn quick and I always got my sense of humor to help me git along with folks. Let me know whut you thank about all this. I know hit's all happening quick, but I miss you terrible. Until I hear from you. I remain yore dutiful servant.

Til Miss Amelia's kitchen sinks,

Clem

The Answer is "Yes"

March 26, 2003

Dearest Clem,

I am literally breathless with emotion. In my wildest imagination I never would have expected anyone to do such a noble thing. Obviously, you have decided to give me this gift without a second thought and I don't know how to react. It is so generous that I don't have the words to convey my gratitude. Simply put...I am overwhelmed! And I would only accept it on the terms that you will be my partner, not only in marriage, but the business, also. We will operate it together like we will be together in all things. You will never have to worry about my leaving you at the altar as Delilah did, for my heart belongs only to you, my dearest Clem.

As you have gathered by now, my answer is "Yes" to your marriage proposal. I cannot wait to see you and your family again. What fun your mother and I will have planning for the wedding, which I would want to happen in Hogwallow. I know it will be the finest wedding that small hamlet has ever seen. I would like for your musical friends to play for the wedding and invite everyone, including dear Jake, whom I hear has gotten his job back with your father's help, and even Burl can put aside his differences long enough to attend. I know your father won't care, even though Burl has filed to reclaim the land he once owned. Your father has shown more than once that good will triumph over the Burl Poindexters of the world.

I have talked to the editors of **Designing Women** and they are transferring me to their office in Fayetteville, so I will be able to manage the restaurant and carry on my duties with Designing Women as well. I don't know what the future holds. If I find that my dual careers is interfering with time I want to spend with you, I will not hesitate to give up my position with the magazine. My desire has always been to cook with the finest chefs in the world and our restaurant will provide me that opportunity. Yes, I would even want to include a delicacy such as possum on the menu. I'm not sure our chefs will know what to do with it, but we can call in your mother on this one.

I have told my mother and father of your good fortune and of your proposal of marriage. I believe that my mother is less hesitant to offer her blessings now that she knows you are wealthy. I know that sounds awful, but her gauge of a person's success is what he has gained materially. I don't agree and I think that in time both my mother and my father will see your good qualities and love you for them. They are a little hesitant about going to Hogwallow for the wedding. Naturally, they prefer that it be held at their country club in Raleigh, but I have told them in no uncertain terms that they will be traveling to Arkansas for this wedding. I will have to send my cousin, former President Bill Clinton, an invitation. I believe that he loves a "hoe down" as much as anyone else. So don't be surprised if he shows up. I'm sure your father will have a lot of questions to ask him about running a political office, and maybe your father can give him some advice about running a successful marriage.

My birthday is on April the second and I do so wish I could be in Hogwallow to celebrate it with your family, but, alas, it is not to be. There are so many things that I must do here in preparation for my trip to your small hamlet. I will drink a glass of champagne for each of us. Now, all that is left is for me to plan for my transfer to Arkansas. I do not want to impose on your parents, so I will find a small apartment in Fayetteville until we can locate a place of our own. I look forward to a new beginning with my husband and our new business. I miss you terribly and anxiously await to hear from you.

With all my love until I see you again,

Amelia

Wedding Plans

April 1, 2003

Dear Miss Amelia,

Yore letter was met with smiles all around here at the Clodhopper household. I can't believe we are gitting married here in Hogwaller. I was afraid that we would have to take Maw to the big city of New York, and iffen I knows Maw she would have gone but she would not have been happy. We want to try and keep Maw happy.

Brother Johnson has been tolt about the wedding, and he will be performing the ceremony. He's already gitting thangs from the Bible to throw into the ceremony, and Sister Johnson is cleaning up the church fer the wedding, which will be, of course, the First Footwashing Baptist Church of the Second Coming of Hogwaller. Paw made the announcement of the marriage in church last Sunday and hit was a big sensation. Burl had to take Delilah home fer she had the vapors and got all weepy, don't you know. Somebody said the Widow Plumlee jist fainted dead away. I guess they were jist happy fer us. Paw invited everyone to the wedding so there hain't no need to send out invitations here. Two thangs that folks don't miss around here are weddings and funerals and sometimes hit's hard to tell which is a'goin' on.

Maw says that you will not be staying at some hotel in Fayetteville. She says they won't know how to feed you and take care of you afore the wedding, being strangers and all. She wants you to stay with her and Paw so's you and her can plan thangs together and not be having to run back and forth from one place to another. Maw has come up with an invitation whut I am sending you to consider. She says hit is jist one example and you can make out one and we'll mull hit over when you gits here. Here is her choice.

Mr. and Missus Jack Blythe

Are asking you all to come and be present at the impairing

nuptials of their daughter

Amelia Winslow

To

Mr. Clem Clodhopper

Son of Clayton and Clara May Clodhopper

Sunday, the 15th of May

At three o'clock

The First Footwashing Baptist Church of the

Second Coming of Hogwaller

Hogwaller, Arkansaw

Y'all Come

Maw knows this may not suit you since you are a big city writer so's we will wait and let you draw one up afore we decides. Maw ain't never been involved in a shindig where there is so much planning to do, so she is looking forward to yore gitting here to holp her in the planning.

Miss Amelia, I am shore sorry that I can't be with you to share yore birthday. Hit ain't no fun alone, so you needs to git out with friends and have a good time. The next birthday you have we will do hit up right at yore fancy restaurant. Until we can do that, this poem I writ fer you will have to do. I knows I'm not Henry Longfeller, but I can throw some words together that ain't half bad. So here's my poem. I hope you likes hit.

Clem's Birthday Card to Miss Amelia

It's yore birthday; since yore my gal
Jist what else could I do?
I had to write a romantical poem
And mail hit off to you.

Now I thought real hard (My hand still hurts)
Fer a rhyme to fit this day;
But to tell the truth, fer a man of words
I don't know whut to say.

I've thought a lot about whut you've got,
Yore looks, and brains, and schooling.
I've writ them down here in this poem
So's you'll know that I ain't fooling.

First of all, I admire yore wit;
It's sharp as an old plowshare.
Them brain doctors need to check yore head;
No telling whut's up there.

And when it comes to having beauty,
You could make a statue cry;
In the *Plowboy Magazine* that I bought,
You looks like Miss July.

And yore sense of humor is right keen;
I laugh until I'm blue
Old Jay Leno on that late night show
Is a hack compared to you.

Don't worry about gitting old and all;
Them wrinkles will have to wait.
Yore jist a babe when I thank back
On them hill wimmen I used to date.

Hair blonde as corn silk in summer sun,
Yore eyes beyond compare;
And when yore setting next to me,
My heart burns with the sweetest fire.

There ain't no downside to yore life;
Yore perfect in ever way.
And afore I finish this birthday card,
I have one last thang to say.

I know I'm just a country boy;
I've seed bad times on the farm,
But I shore got a bumper crop
The day that you were born.

I know hit's a tad rough, but I'll git better because I plans on writing a lot of thangs fer you. I know yore busy with all the moving, so's I'll let you git back to hit. I love you more than a tick on a hound dog.

Yore financee,

Clem

Hello, Hogwallow

April 6, 2003

My dearest Clem,

It appears that plans are proceeding nicely there. I should be there within the week if all goes as I believe it will here. Yes, of course, I will stay with Clayton and Clara May if that is their wish. I did not want to be a bother, but it would be better for the planning of the wedding. Of course, you must be the perfect gentleman and allow me time to prepare for this wonderful day. I will not have time to sit and hold hands and take long walks and say loving words as I wish we could do. It will be a busy time for us all. I will not have time to sneak away on my second night there to a secluded spot on the river. And the dinner that I will prepare and place strategically in your house is not for us to eat if we should sneak away on that second night. Because, as I said, I will be very busy. After all, we must be very proper. As you know, many eyes will be upon us.

Clem, I love your mother very much, but I will indeed have to make some changes to the invitations. I do not wish to do it for myself, but my parents would be very upset if the invitations were not done to their satisfaction. It would be better for all of us if my mother were not homicidal when she attends the ceremony. I will print out an example and bring it with me. I do hope that your mother understands. Please inform Mrs. Johnson that I fully expect to help with the decoration of the church. In fact, I must insist upon it for the sake of all of us. I have mentioned that my mother will be attending, did I not? With the number of friends and relatives she will be bringing, it would be wise to consider holding the wedding outside if the weather is good. Again, it is something I wish to talk over with your parents and Brother and Sister Johnson when I get there. Everything must be just so. There is the slightest of chances that former President Bill Clinton, who is my cousin, will attend. If that were to happen, naturally, the press would need accommodations as well as camera crews. I hope this is not sounding like an extravagant affair because I know how important it is to you to feel comfortable. I know it sounds as if I am asking to be a big part of the planning, but did I say my mother will be there?

Thank you so much for my beautiful birthday poem. I will treasure it and keep it close to read over and over again until I see you. Everything is proceeding nicely here though it is quite a strain on my time and my energy. However, when I think of you, I find renewed fortitude and forge ahead undaunted by any obstacles that might impede my hastening to your side. Yet, for now, I must close and tend to many pressing matters. Look for me within the week. As ever, I am your Amelia.

With unfailing devotion,

Amelia

Oil's Well That Ends Well

April 11, 2003

Dear Miss Amelia,

Since you will be here to stay in a few days, this will be the last letter to come out of these hills. I ain't much on writing and since you will be here, there won't be no need no more. You will have to admit that I'se gotten better over the months we has been writing to each other. A lot has been happening in a hurry here and I will tell you all about it, so jist sit down and hang on.

First, Maw is fine with you gitting them invitations done. She hain't had much experience, so's she will jist leave hit up to you. She knows how maws are all over the world, and she wants yores to have a good time whilst she's here. She did git a little perturbed when she heered that former President Clinton might be here. She didn't vote for him, don't you know, and she's a little skeered that he will remember that she voted fer Gore. The second time he run, she didn't even vote. She said if people hain't got no more sense than to vote for him once, then they's going to vote for him twice, so why go to the voting place? She has better thangs to do. Maw's funny that way. Paw thanks that it would be a hoot to meet a former President of the United States. He says he can talk over politicks with him and pick his brain about what Hogwaller needs.

Brother Johnson agrees that if the weather ain't bad that hit would be a good idea to have the wedding outside the church because there is going to be a whole passel of people showing up. All one hundred or so of Hogwaller will be here as well as most people in Hootin' Holler because they'se heered that former President Clinton might be here. The radio and television people have been calling, and some of them will be here. I don't know if there will be room fer all these folks even if we holds it outside. I have to admit that I'se gitting a little skittish and am looking forward to yore coming so's you can help me settle down. Maw and Paw ain't helpful a'tall. Maw is organizing the ladies and picking the scarves and hats and outfits that they will wear. Paw is organizing a welcoming group in case Mr. Clinton does show up. Paw says they will give him the key to the city if he can find hit. Why there ain't been this many excited people since Bill Nutley got drunk and ran nekked through the town whilst they was having the St. Patrick's parade. They wasn't nothing but two floats and Lester Bumpkus's John Deere tracter, so Bill's entrance drew the most cheers of all. He had painted hisself all green and had nothing on but his birthday suit. Granny Johnson, the preacher's grandmaw, said she could see why his wife left him. He didn't have a thang she would be interested in. Anyways, folks are a'keeping their eyes out fer Bill jist in case he decides to make another run. We don't want to embarrass Hogwaller with so many highlanders here. They'se apt to thank we don't have no culture a'tall.

With all the other doings going on, you would thank that thangs couldn't git more exciting. Wal, git this. You knows I was a'telling you about Lawyer Bumpkus who Burl hired to sue Paw to git his land back and who is the brother to Lester Bumpkus who has the green John Deere tracter whut was in the St. Patrick's parade where Bill Nutley ran through the town nekked? You know how thoughtful and generous Paw is to everybody and how he's always trying to do the right thang? Paw and Maw was sitting and talking the other night about all the money they was going to be a'gitting and what they should do with it. They already has more than they will ever need, and more will be coming in fer a long time. Paw has decided that the town of Hogwaller should share in the wealth. He is going to give every citizen in Hogwaller a interest in the well. They'se only about a hunderd adults in the whole town, so all of them will come into a passel of money. Even Burl and his boys will git their shares. Since they'se so many of them, they will do right well. It works out fine because since Burl will be gitting more money than he has seed in his life, he is dropping the case against Paw, and Lawyer Bumpkus is fit to be tied. Delilah is already figgering how she can git to New York and start her cookie and candy business with her money. Jake is going to retire from the post office and rest his toe. The little Ledbetter boy who had his eyes crost and couldn't see a lick is going to git an operation to fix his eyes. They'se a lot of good thangs the money will do fer the residents of Hogwaller. The only worry I have is that all this money will change the people here. They'se not used to having so much at one time and, human nature being whut it is, I'm afraid Hogwaller will change fer the worser. I don't thank Maw and Paw will ever change, and I'm mighty thankful fer that. You and me will be moving to the big city of Fayetteville and I won't git to see the people here much, but I don't reckon I'll change unless it's fer the better because you will be there to help me. I'll learn to talk better and write better and believe more in myself because you care about me. So all them changes will be good ones. Life fer both of us will change. But I know enough to say that if we loves each other, nothing else ain't going to matter. I struck my own oil well when I fount you and that's more important than all the gold in the world.

Now all that's left is to prepare fer the wedding. Yore going to be surprised at how busy this little town is while gitting ready fer yore arrival. It seems like a lifetime since I first writ to you fer advice on how to cook a possum and now we is gitting married. Who knowed that a possum would brang us together? Jake came by today to thank Paw fer his kindness and fer helping him to git his job back though he allows he will retire with his share in the gas well. It is right fitting to send you this pitcher of Jake. When you sees hit, I knows you will laugh. I will close and I knows I will see you soon. Here's the pitcher of Jake and his friend.

Yores forever.

Clem.

The End

Epilogue: Part One

Night had fallen on this sleepy little hamlet nestled in the hills outside of Fayetteville, Arkansas. The full moon cast a silvery glow over the landscape and if one listened carefully, he could hear the distant sound of a train whistle which carried over the ridges and valleys and dissipated into the night. But other than its fading soliloquy, no sound disturbed the quietness of the evening. The remoteness of the area was punctuated by only one house, a modest dwelling constructed in a Cape Cod style more suited to Maine than Arkansas. From one dimly lighted window came the sound of music. It was not the classical sounds of Vivaldi or Beethoven, nor some renowned operatic tenor of the day which one would expect to hear emanating from a home whose inhabitants obviously were of good taste and character, but a country piece replete with banjo, guitars, fiddles, and the nasal twang of one of the aspiring country artists one so often hears in cities like Nashville or Memphis. A small lamp perched on the corner of a desk outlined a solitary figure who sat reflectively, working quietly and deliberately on a piece of paper in front of him. It was obvious that the writer struggled with the words that he laboriously scribbled on the sheet as if each syllable were a bramble in a field of briars that he must wade through. The house was quiet and the hour was late, yet the solemn figure remained steadfastly pondering the white stationery in front of him. Occasionally, as if struck by some unknown muse, he feverishly scribbled notes onto the pad. He was thus occupied when a figure appeared behind him and placed a delicate hand upon his shoulder. The sudden appearance of the woman startled him momentarily and he turned in the chair to greet his visitor.

"Clem, what are you doing up so late? You know we have to rise early if we are going to meet the Capshaws tomorrow and finalize the papers on the restaurant."

"Hit's only nine o'clock, Miss Amelia. I'se working on New York Time instead of Hogwaller time."

"Don't give me any of your folksy rationalization. You've rarely been up past 8:30 in your life. I want you to be sharp when we start doing business."

"Wal, you know I ain't got no head fer money figgering. Hain't that whut lawyers are fer?"

"I suppose you're right. There won't be much to do other than sign a million papers. But what has you so engrossed that it is keeping you up so late?"

"I'se writing a letter to my cousin who lives close to Little Rock. You remembers I got this letter from him Tuesday week and he were real sorry that he couldn't come to the wedding. I tolt you that he had jist gone through his fifth wife and were in no mood to see anuther man suffer the same fate he had fer so many times."

"This cousin seems to have a very grim view of marriage. Which cousin is this? It seems you have hundreds scattered about."

"His name is Rastus Foggybottom and he lives so fur back in the hills that they has to send his mail by carrier pigeon. Rastus is real sorry he couldn't come to see us git hitched, being that I is his favorite cuzzin and all. But they is finalizing his papers so's he can git rid of Mabel. He says she is making his life awful with her nagging ways. Of course, they's two sides to ever circle. Rastus ain't the easiest person to git along with. Howsomeever, having said that, two of them failures waren't Rastus' fault. Two of his wifes died in untimely fashion, don't you know."

"Oh, my goodness, Clem!" Two of his wives died?"

"Hit were tragic, but most of Rastus's life has been tragic. His first wife were good enuff, but hit didn't take Beulah long to find out Rastus waren't husband material. She give him a year to see iffen he was as bad as he seemed, and shore enuff he were. Beulah were the reforming type, but in Rastus she could see he was a cat who couldn't be skint, so she jist give up. So's one year was all hit lasted."

"Then he met Arlene and that lasted two years so he were a'making progress, but when Rastus dranks a mite, he gits mean and Arlene jist couldn't put up with a mean drunk. Rastus come home one night drunk as usual and when Arlene started in on one of her lectures, hit jist plumb struck Rastus the wrong way and he slapped Arlene. Wal, that was that. Her paw came with a shotgun the next day and only Arlene's pleading kept Rastus frum leaving this world with a hide full of buck shot. So that ended his second marriage."

"His third wife Jolene lasted only four months but it waren't Rastus's fault because she died sudden like. Hit seems that she were up on the roof a'putting shingles on. She had jist stopped because hit

154

had started to rain and when she stepped on the ladder rung, hit were slick and she fell off and broke her neck. Rastus were real sorry about the whole thang and blamed hisself fer not being up on the roof and breaking his neck instead of hern. Of course, everbidy in the Clodhopper fambly knows Rastus can't stand being on high places. Hit's one of them phobias you've heered about called clutzyphobia. I don't know whut phobia hit is fer not fixing the porch when hit needed work, but hit seems he had that'un too. Anyways, Rastus give her a fine funeral and moved on to number four."

"I never got to know Pauline much. Rastus got acquainted with Pauline by gitting on one of them dating services. He figgered he stood a better chance of gitting a gal iffen she didn't see him up close fer a while, so's he had a friend of hissen to go on one of them dating services on the computer. That'un worked out fer Rastus better'n all them otherns. Hit seems that Rastus had used a pitcher of his cousin Zeb to send to her. Zeb is purty good looking and hit seemed the best thang to do since Rastus hain't much to look at. Wal, hit seems that Pauline had did the same thang. So's when they finally met up, they had a good laugh about hit. Both were as ugly as sin, but Rastus loved her and they got along swell. Pauline got with child and Rastus were as happy as a fox in a hen house until complications set in and she died afore the baby were born. Rastus took that awful hard."

"I thank he married Mabeline on one of them rebound thangs where he needed somebody to git him over Pauline's passing. Mabeline's paw is a Southern Baptist preacher and he tried to reform Rastus. Hit seemed to be working fer a while, but Rastus ain't one to make a habit out of anythang but dranking, and he shore waren't going to make a habit of going to church. Hit became a sore point to Mabeline's folks, Mabeline made the mistake of joining with her maw and paw in trying to git Rastus to join the church and quit dranking, and cussing, and smoking and all them other vices whut Rastus enjoys so much until he jist decided that he'd ruther be single than nagged to death. So's now he is gitting unhitched from Mabeline and he waren't in no mood to go to no wedding."

"Five marriages! My goodness, Clem. What would you two have in common? You are so wonderful that I can't ever imagine us not being together for the rest of our lives."

"Hit's one of them man thangs where's he can't git along with wimmen but he's comfortable around his own kind."

155

"His own kind? You mean other men? Well, if he likes you, he can't be too bad. What are you writing to him about?"

"He wanted fer me to tell him about all the wedding going ons whut went on at our wedding. Rastus is as big a gossip as ary woman. Excuse me, Miss Amelia. Yore an exception. He jist wants to know whut all the folks did because I'se told him so much about Hogwaller."

"Yes, I imagine he would love your stories. Write your letter, but come to bed soon. You know how I like to snuggle in close to you. It helps me sleep."

"I'll be there in two shakes of old Buford's tail."

Rastus Foggybottom
Possum Holler
Box 21
Little Rock, Arkansaw

Dear Rastus,

Wal, you wanted to heer about the wedding so strap yoreself into a cheer and hang on. Hit were the most commotion I has seed since Joe Spivey got drunk and drove his truck into the local Alcoholiks Anunamus meetings there in Hogwaller. Hit seems that Joe was a'goin' to the meeting that night fer the second time. He had been sober fer two days and he felt he needed to celebrate the occasion, so's he stopped in at the Broken Leg Saloon to have jist a snort afore the meeting. You've heered of them steps that alcoholiks has to go through. Wal, Joe had figgered you needed to brace yoreself to face them steps, so he had jist enuff to calm his nerves, which were about a bottle of Jim Beam. When he arrived at the meeting, he were a little foggy and overshot his landing which wound him and the truck up smack in the middle of the meeting purty much on time. I thank they kicked him out and tolt him not to come back until he were a mite more serious in his intentions. Anyways, whut I am going to tell you about the wedding puts Joe's antics to shame.

Hit's the day afore the wedding when I first meets Miss Amelia's folks. They arrives in this big, long car whut takes up most of the yard at my folk's place. When they pulls in, Miss Amelia runs out to meet them and they's jist falling all over each other with happiness. Of course, Maw and Paw goes out to meet them and invites them in. When Mrs. Blythe comes into the house, she looks around and this look comes into her eyes whut tolt me she were impressed by whut she seed. Maw had been cleaning fer two days gitting ready fer Amelia's folks to come and visit. Now with Amelia staying at her house, Maw knowed it would be hard to let her folks stay there, too. That would be too much a strain on relations that close to the wedding. So Paw had checked with Mrs. Watkins who lives down the road a spell who keeps one of them bed and breakfast places. Hit's never full cause we don't git that many people here in Hogwaller. So's they would like hit fine. But Maw still wanted to impress them with her housewife skills and she had outdone herself. I know Mrs. Blythe had never seed anythang like hit. She took off that little bonnet she had on her head and started to fanning herself to beat the band and this pale look come over her face. Mr. Blythe steddied her by gitting a'holt of her arm and leading her to a cheer. Maw felt real bad fer putting on airs and thought mebbe that Missus Blythe wuz jist overcome by all the fine housekeeping she had seed.

Well, Maw tells them to make theirselves at home and she will git some of her sweet tea. Maw's sweet tea is knowed all over Hogwaller as being the best. So she gits some Mason jars out of the cupboard and pours some sweet tea and gives hit to Amelia's folks. Now, Mrs. Blythe looks at them jars like she can't believe whut she is a'seein'. But she takes a sip of Maw's tea, and a strange looks comes over her face. She takes another'un and a little smile comes upon her face. She takes a big swaller and that smile gits bigger. Maw is jist on pins and needles, but she pertends she hain't watching fer a reaction. When Mrs. Blythe tells her hit's the best she ever drunk, hit made Maw's day. After that, thangs seemed to loosen up a mite. Maw's sweet tea will do that. Hit don't hurt that a little of Rufus's shine is part of the ingredients, nuther. Of course we didn't tell Mrs. And Mr. Blythe about the moonshine. By the time they left to go to the bed and breakfast place, Maw and Paw and Amelia's folks was jist like old friends. Hit seemed to take a load offen Miss Amelia's shoulders to see them git along.

Wal, Rastus, Miss Amelia wants me to come to bed, so's I'll close fer now. After we meet them real estate folks tomorry to close on the restaurant, I'll write agin and give details on the wedding.

As ever, I am yore cuzzin Clem

Epilogue: Part Two

Rastus Foggybottom
Possum Holler
Box 21
Little Rock, Arkansaw

Dear Cuzzin Rastus,

I'se going to continue telling you about the wedding in this here letter, and whut a wedding hit was! Miss Amelia will jist take off a'laffing ever time she thanks about hit. I know hit were a special occasion fer her and I'll thank you'll see why after I tells you some of the going's on that was a'goin' on.

First thang on our wedding day Maw gits everbidy up at six o'clock in the morning. Miss Amelia didn't seem none too happy about gitting up that early, but Maw says the early bird gits the worm and they's people to feed and thangs to git ready and folks to meet. Maw had tolt me to stay away because I waren't allowed to see Miss Amelia until the ceremonial riots, so I jist took old Buford fer a little hunt about daybreak to stiddy my nerves. The ceremony is to be at three o'clock that afternoon, so's about ten o'clock thangs start popping.

I never knows whut is going on and hit were the same with the wedding plans. They jist tells me to show up and be ready to say "I do" when the preacher asks me iffen I does. So when Miss Amelia tolt me about some of the thangs she had been a'doin' fer her part, I has to admit I was a little surprised. Hit seems that as soon as Miss Amelia got to Hogwaller from New York, she started meeting with folks and planning the wedding. I'se learnt never to be surprised at whut a woman does, but git this. Miss Amelia had gone to Maw and asked her to be the matron of honor, which thrilled Maw to no end. Then she went to Delilah and the Widow Plumlee and asked them to be bridesmaids, which they agreed to do although the Widow Plumlee teared up with joy and cried fer a spell. I can't figger whut all the fuss is about. Paw is going to be my best man and I got some of Burl's boys to holp me out and I'se ready to go. But wimmen make such a fuss about gitting married and after they's married, they make a fuss about everthang else. But Miss Amelia is an exception.

Wal, I tolt you to take a seat and hang on. Here's whut happened first thang. Hit's about ten thirty in the morning and people are already standing around and eyeballing everthang. They's news folks everwhar and Paw is in heaven. He's talking to folks and telling some of his favorite jokes which Maw has checked to make shore they'se clean, and he's taking the news folk on a tour of the town which don't take much time. Burl and his boys have camped out under a big shade tree and air jist a'waitin' fer the show to start. Hit seems that everbidy in Hogwaller and Hootin Holler has showed up and hit's still four hours til the wedding. Nobidy wants to miss anythang. This is the biggest social event that Hogwaller has ever seed and nobidy wanted to be left out. Hit's jist driving Maw crazy because she's trying to git Miss Amelia settled down so's she can git her make up and wedding duds on. The news folks has staked out the house so that iffen Bill Clinton showed up, they'd be able to git some good pitchers.

Then thangs started to happen in a hurry. Suddenly, three of the biggest dang vehickles I'se ever seed pulls up at the church. You knows, of course, our church Is The First Footwashing Baptist Church of the Second Coming of Hogwaller. Wal, these cars pulls up, and six big men jumps out and starts running around like chickins with their heads chopped off. They'se got sunglasses on and dark suits and ever one of them old boys is as big as Clovis and twice as mean looking. They station themselves around and starts talking on them cell phones to somebidy. Them press people seem to know whut is happening and they rushes toward them cars. About that time another car pulls up, dust a'flying. Then hit happened. You know how hit's always calmest afore a storm and how three people can keep a secret iffen two of them folks are dead? You kin see whut I'm a'gittin' at. They was an axident that happened right in front of the church. Hit seems the little Ledbetter boy was hit by that last car. You remembers the Ledbetter boy who has the crost eyes and whut wanders around a lot because he can't git his eyes uncrost? He is going to git an operation on the money from Paw's gas well, but he hain't done hit yit. So's he's jist meandering around and stumbles into the path of that car. Hit clips him and knocks him a'winding even more than he already is and everbidy jist goes quiet and nobidy seems to know whut to do. Then that car door opens and hit's Bill Clinton hisself. He hustles over to the

160

little Ledbetter boy and lifts him up and takes him over to a table and signals fer somebidy to git help. One of them men comes over and checks the boy out and he seems satisfied that the Ledbetter boy is alright. Jist shaken up a mite. He opens his eyes and looks around and hit's almost like a miracle. The boy's eyes ain't crost a'tall. He's looking straight ahead as purty as you please. Now in all the commotion, everbidy has jist plumb forgot that hit's Bill Clinton a'standin' there holding the boy. The little Ledbetter boy gits down and walks forward to meet his Maw and he's straight as any arrow. His maw starts in to crying and Grandmaw Johnson says hit's a miracle and Bill performed hit. Wal, I ain't going to say he did or he didn't, but hit shore created some excitement. Paw said Bill done more good for the Ledbetter boy than he did the whole time he were in office. Of course, he said hit to me under his breath, so's Maw wouldn't heer. I ain't a religious man as you knows, but I was a mite shaken up when I seed the Ledbetter boy walking in a straight line thataway. Hit jist goes to show you that fate kin take a'holt of you and cause you all kinds of misery or, on the tother hand, hit kin straighten out yore eyeballs.

Then suddenly everbidy jist gasped because a lady steps out of the limosine and hit's Hillary. She's come to the wedding with Bill, and now everbidy is jist falling all over each other with excitement and them old boys with the sunglasses is a'pushing everbidy back as they tries to git close to Bill and Hillary. The press is a'snappin' away with them cameras and trying to git close fer good shots. Hillary is jist smiling as purty as you please but she seems a little worried fer Bill because Delilah has cornered him and give him some of her cakes and candies which he seems right happy to git. Delilah was never one to miss an oppertunity to better herself and she shore waren't goin to miss this'un. Delilah's cookies and candies must have made quite an impression because we fount out later that Bill offered her a job with his cooking staff. So Delilah has made hit after all. Now Bill can have some of Delilah's donuts and cookies and candies anytime he wants them. Maw thanks that Hillary appeared a mite jealous, but all maws thank that most wimmen are jealous. Paw says that Hillary mite be jealous of Bill's success. After all, she's jist a secretary. Paw can't figger out why she would jist give up a job as one of them senators to be one of them typers. Hit jist ain't logical he says.

Paw and Sheriff Tate and them sunglass fellers finally gits Bill and Hillary excavated from out among them folks and takes them into the mayor's office where's they can git some peace fer a while. The press people set up camp outside the office jist waiting fer them to come out. Wal, Hillary decides hit might be a good time to git some votes in case she gives up her secretary job and wants to be President. So she steps outside with them sunglass fellers all around her and starts to telling the folks about how Bill growed up in their great state and went on to be President and he never forgit who put him there and that's the reason they are there today. She were jist a smiling and waving and talking when whut we feered would happen happened. You remembers how I were a'telling you in another letter how Bill Nutley got drunk on Saint Patrick's Day and painted hisself green and ran nekked through town in the parade whut had only two floats and Lester Bumpkus's green John Deere tracter and how Granny Johnson, the preacher's grandmaw, said she could see why his wife left him because he didn't have a thang she wanted? Wal, hit happened agin. Yep, Bill showed up and he were nekked as a plucked chickin agin. Only this time he weren't green and hit weren't St. Patrick's Day. When Hillary saw Bill nekked, she nearly had the vapors and had to be holped back into the office. Wal, the tother Bill stepped out of the office to see whut were a'goin' on and he got an eyeful as nekked Bill were sprinting away. Lack I said, he weren't green but he left everbidy a message because he painted hit on his butt cheeks. Hit read "Party" on one butt cheek and "Nekked" on the tother. Now even President Bill got to laughing when he read hit. Paw says he jist hopes that President Clinton don't thank that everbidy in Hogwaller is as crazy as Bill Nutley.

Now after Bill turnt the corner and everbidy had settled down, I thought that everthang would be smoother than butter, but when hit rains hit pours. Bill and Hillary had got back into their car to drive to Paw's house to see Amelia. Of course, Amelia don't know a thang about them being there, so she's jist gitting dressed and doing thangs to git ready fer the wedding. Bill and Hillary is rolling right along when suddenly the car stops so quickly that hit nearly throws them into the front seat. When they looks out the window, they sees Granny Birdwell driving her cow to be milked, and hit had stopped in the middle of the road and were chewing some sweet grass. Wal, Granny don't know Bill Clinton from Bill Nutley, and she can't see too good anyways, so's she jist lets the cow eat and sits down on the side of the road. She figgered Old Lulu was a'goin to do whut she wanted to and so would she. A couple of them big old boys whut wears the sunglasses gits out and looks at that cow like hit's a alien. They tries to shush hit out of the road, but hit ain't shushing. Granny could have tolt them hit were useless to try and move a cow iffen she don't want moved. They see they hain't making no progress so's they finds a stick and starts to hitting her on the rump and I hain't never knowed of a cow gitting so perturbed. She turns around and starts a'mooin' and a'shakin' her head and runs right at them guys with the sticks. They's ducking and dodging so Lulu takes aim at the car and butts hit a couple of times. By that time the driver was beating a hasty retreat on up the road and Bill and Hillary were safe fur the moment. You know how Paw is. When he fount out whut had happened, he jist laughed and said that Old Lulu was the closest thang that Hogwaller had to a terrorist.

Anyways, the Clintons made hit safely to Paw's house and decided hit would be best iffen they jist stayed there until the wedding. Of course, Maw had to give them some sweet tea out of them Mason jars. You remembers whut I tolt you about Rufus's shine being one of the makings? Wal, after about three glasses, Bill were looking a little flushed and Hillary was asking Maw fer her recipe fer chicken and dumplin's. Amelia were too excited to talk. To have the Clintons at her wedding was the most exciting thang whut she had ever knowed.

Wal, that's about all I can write today. Hit takes a spell to write down whut I want to say and Miss Amelia gits a little peeved iffen I'm up too late. I'll tell you about the actual wedding in my next letter.

Until then, I remain yore Cuzzin,
Clem

163

Epilogue: Part Three

Rastus Foggybottom
Possum Holler
Box 21
Little Rock, Arkansaw

Dear Cuzzin Rastus,

Wal, when I left you last time, Bill and Hillary had arrived at Maw and Paw's house and had some of Maw's sweet tea and were a'feeling' purty good. Amelia were jist beside herself with excitement that her Cuzzin Bill had made hit to the wedding. Of course, I'm out hunting with Old Buford and trying to stiddy my nerves afore the wedding. Me and Old Buford ain't heered all the goin's on whut had been a'goin' on in town.

Hit's about two o'clock and I tells Old Buford we needs to head back and git ready fer the wedding. Wal, don't you know that the first thang that happens is Old Buford sees a fox and takes off after hit jist a'howlin' like all git out. He's jist a'barrelin' along and comes to the old Barlow place whut is abandoned. Jist as hit looks like he might git that fox, Old Buford disappears from sight in a cloud of dust. First, he's a'runnin' and then he ain't to be seed. When I gits to the spot whar he disappeared, they's a big hole whut used to be a well and he's fell into hit. I can hear him jist carryin' on down in that hole but hit's a deep'un and I can't git to him. Hit's jist a reverse of them Lassie movies whar Timmy falls into the well and Lassie has to git help. I tells old Buford to jist hold on and I'll be back with help and I takes off a'runnin'.

When I gits to Maw and Paw's house, they's jist leaving fer the church with Amelia and Bill and Hillary. I rushes in and tells them whut has happened and Bill is real sorry. Hit seems like he used to hunt when he was a boy and likes a good dog as well as the next person. Amelia is all dressed up as purty as you will ever see, but she says she's a'goin' with us. We head out and git to the Barlow place quicker than a hiccup. Wal, old Buford is a'howlin' and a'carryin' on something awful. Paw is the smallest man there so he volunteers to go down into the hole and brang Buford out. We ties a rope around him and them old sunglass boys lowers him down into the hole until we heers him yell that he's fount Buford. We raises them up out of the hole and Old Buford is a mess. He's purty tore up whar he was scratched and bruised by rocks when he fell. He was bleeding purty bad out of one of them gashes and we didn't have no bandages. Now git this. Miss Amelia takes her gown and rips out the bottom of hit to use for bandages for Buford. Right then, I knowed that I would love her forever. We patched Buford up as best we could and took him back into town. He was going to be alright, but hit were four o'clock and the wedding folk didn't know whut had happened. Brother Johnson had entertained them with some jokes, and parables, and sich but they was gittin' a tad restless when we showed up.

I got my wedding duds on as quick as I could, but Miss Amelia's gown were a mess. She knowed she couldn't git married in hit and she jist started to cry. Wal, leave hit to a woman to come up with a answer when hit comes to wedding problems. Hillary said Amelia could wear one of her outfits in the wedding. They's about the same size so hit would work. Now Hillary has several outfits like she is seed wearing in the news like them pants outfits, don't you know, but Miss Amelia settles on a dress she likes and puts hit on. She couldn't have looked more beautifuller. Hit ain't the clothes that make the woman, but the woman who makes the clothes is the way I figgers hit.

Anyways there ain't no wedding gown parlors where a person kin git a dress on short notice, so Miss Amelia says hit would be an honor to wear one of Hillary's dresses. She puts hit on and she is the most beautifullest thang whut I had ever seed. We heads on over to the church and git there jist as Brother Johnson is gitting through with a story whut tolt about how them kings in the Old Testament had all them wifes and how today you can't have but one wife and you needs to be shore she's a good'un before you gits hitched. I knows I got a good'un and I was right anxious to git started.

Then hit starts. The organist hits that "here comes the bride" and everbidy turns around to see Miss Amelia and her paw come down the isle. When they gits to the alter, Miss Amelia's paw seems to not want to let go of Miss Amelia's hand, but she kisses him on the jaw and he goes and sets down by Missus Blythe. Everthang starts out good with Brother Johnson telling about how marriage is a sacred institution and hit should not be got into lightly. Mr. and Missus Clinton are jist sitting and smiling there on the front row. The Ledbetter boy has a special place beside Mr. Clinton and Hillary. Mr. Clinton can't seem to take his eyes offen Delilah who is the purtiest woman thar cept fer Miss Amelia. I knows he is thanking about how she is going to make more of them pies and cakes fer him. Old Jake has been given a special place up front since his toes were twinging him a tad. Even the possum on his shoulder seemed to be smiling. Well, as I sed, thangs were going as smooth as goose grease when all of a sudden Bill Nutley appcared agin. Jist as Brother Johnson were a'askin' iffen anybidy had any just cause why me and Miss Amelia should not be jined in holy matrimony, Bill came a'runnin' down the aisle and planted a big kiss on Missus Clinton's lips. Wal, then hit all broke loose. The sunglasses fellers is all over Bill like a bad case of poison ivy, but they is hesitant to git a good grip since he ain't wearing no clothes. They don't know whut to grab on to and when they hesitate, Bill is gone. Wal, the chase is on and the last thang anybidy sees is Bill a'leadin' them sunglasses fellers acrost the hills. I don't thank they'se going to ketch Bill. He's a lot lighter and in better shape plus he hain't got no clothes to hinder his running. Grandmaw Johnson jist mutters under her breath about how God should have give him less energy and blessed him more in some other places.

Wal, after thangs has settled down, Brother Johnson started in agin and we git to the part where we is to exchange rings. When Paw goes to git the ring out of his pocket, hit ain't there. In all the excitement of having Bill and Hillary at his house, he forgot to put the ring in his coat. Miss Amelia looks like she is going to cry and Maw rushes forward and takes her ring off and gives hit to me and I place hit on Miss Amelia's fanger. So Miss Amelia starts off her marriage with two borried items, a dress from Miss Hillary and Maw's wedding ring. With all the going's on, a feller would thank Miss Amelia would be shedding tears ever whichaway, but she don't. Hit seemed that when thangs couldn't git worser, she got tougher. She waren't going to let nothing spile her wedding. She just sed that hit's thangs like nekked Bill that makes an event memorable. I knows I won't fergit hit.

When the "I do's" were done, I kist Miss Amelia smack on the lips and we headed down the isle with everbidy jist hooraying. We gits outside and I'm expecting my old truck to be waiting with old shoes and cans tied to hit, but hit ain't nowhere to be seed. Then from around back of the church we hear a loud roar and the biggest John Deere tracter I have ever seed comes up in front of the church. Paw is sitting on hit as purty as you please and he tells me hit is mine. Hit is all decorated with signs and sich wishing me and Miss Amelia good luck. Paw always knowed that I wanted a house with some land where I could have chickins, and horses, and mules, and cows, and plenty of space fer old Buford to run and hunt. He said I would need a good tracter and this was the biggest and best that John Deere made. I could see Miss Amelia had some doubts about gitting on hit, but she climbed right on.

Afore we took off, Bill and Hillary wished us good luck and said fer us to come visit them after we got back from our honeymoon, which we said we would. Paw shook my hand and Maw climbed up and kist us on the cheek and tolt us to be keerful. I could see Miss Amelia were gitting teary eyed, so I revved up the John Deere and we were off. As we crost the fields to go home to pack fer the honeymoon, the day were waning. The setting sun was jist beautiful and the day had been perfect even with all the going's on going on. I looked over at Miss Amelia who was jist laughing to beat the band and I ast her whut was so funny. She jist pointed to a distant hill and I looked jist in time to ketch a last glimpse of Bill Nutley disappearing over the ridge with those sunglass fellers in pursuit. Hit couldn't have been a better ending.

The End

Our Other Book By This Author

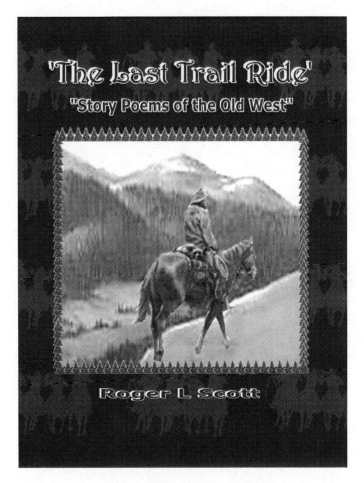

ISBN: 978-1-4092-4373-1

The poems in this book stand as a tribute to those hardy men who once rode the West with just their horse and guns, carving out a civilization and establishing laws where none had existed before. You will enjoy living life as the cowboys did as you read along, experiencing both the joy and the harshness of being out on the Western frontier. These poems open up the world of cowboys, gunslingers, and lawmen…all to show how the West was won through the blood and sweat of those early pioneers.

www.apfppublisher.com

Two More Books By This Author

ISBN: 1-4137-1719-5   **ISBN: 9781413756630**

Both Published by Publish America:

A.P. F.P CHARITY BOOKS

(All done with the help of the Poets World-Wide Group)

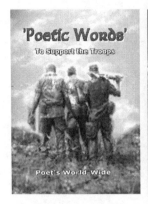  

All Info and details can be found at

www.p.f.p.publishers.com

A P.F.P.AUTHORS AND BOOK TITLES:

Patricia Ann Farnsworth-Simpson: Windows of Light:
Life's Carousel: A Bundle of Muse: The Twinkles:
Flick The Karate Pig: The Wizard the Witch and Joe the Toe:
A Compilation of Tales to Thrill and Chill:
Stories To Thrill and Delight: Jack the Lad:
Carolyn Scuozzo My Garden is Growing:
Christina R Jussaume Amazing Pets & Animals. Spiritual Living
Waters: Jseph's Star Of Eternal Promise:
To God Give The Glory:
Daveda Gruber A Blonde View of Life: More Snapshots:
The Blonde Who Found Jesus: Tales of a Tiny Dog:
Castle of Ice: Lady Godiva:
Erich J Goller The Trojan Horse: Groovy:
Jacquelyn Sturge Live, Love Laugh A Lot:
Live, Love Laugh With me Through Poetry A to Z
J. Elwood Davis The Blue Collar Scholar:
Jennifer Lee Wilson Fantasy and Foibles:
Joe Hartman Pieces of Existence:
Joanne Agee Born To Be A Rebel:
Joree Williams Ariella:
Kathleen Charnes-Zvetkoff Embroidered Limericks:
Michael L Schuh But Its Mine: Mike and Joe: The Cross:
Spiritual Thoughts on Love and Life: The Porter Family:
Poets World-Wide Great Poets 2008 : The Jesters Book:
A Tribute to a Songbird: The Poets Choice Book 2009:
Richard A Rousay Choose the Right and Walk With Noah:
Choose The Right and Walk With Ruth.
Robert Hewett Sr Down The Road We Came:
William Garret & Rochelle Fischer Rosewood:
Poems & Promises: